The Merto

Thomas Merton

THE MERTON PRAYER

An Exercise in Authenticity

STEVEN A. DENNY

Photographs by Stephen L. Hufman

The Merton Prayer
An Exercise in Authenticity
by Steven A. Denny

Edited by Gregory F. Augustine Pierce
Design and typeset by Andrea Reider
Original Part-Two Photographs and Cover Photograph by Stephen L. Hufman, M.D.

"The Merton Prayer," a chapter in *Thoughts in Solitude* (Farrar, Straus, Giroux Publishing, 1956, 1958, 2009) p. 79, is used with permission of FSG.

Photograph of Thomas Merton by John Lyons on page i is used with permission of the Merton Legacy Trust and Thomas Merton Center at Bellarmine University.

Photograph of Thomas Merton by Sibylle Akers on page 151 is used with permission of the Merton Legacy Trust and Thomas Merton Center at Bellarmine University.

Photograph of Thomas Merton's gravesite on page 157 is used with permission of the Merton Legacy Trust and Thomas Merton Center at Bellarmine University.

Scripture quotations are from the *Holy Bible, New Living Translation,* copyright ©1996, 2004, 2015 by Tyndale House Foundation. Used by permission of Tyndale House Publishers, a Division of Tyndale House Ministries, Carol Stream, Illinois 60188. All rights reserved.

Other Scripture translations noted when used:

Scripture quotations marked (NIV) are from the *Holy Bible, New International Version®*, NIV®. Copyright © 1973, 1978, 1984, 2011 by Biblica, Inc.™ Used by permission of Zondervan. All rights reserved worldwide. www.zondervan.com._The "NIV" and "New International Version" are trademarks registered in the United States Patent and Trademark Office by Biblica, Inc.™

Scripture quotations marked KJV are from *The Authorized (King James) Version.* Rights in the Authorized Version in the United Kingdom are vested in the Crown. Reproduced by permission of the Crown's patentee, Cambridge University Press.

Published by ACTA Publications, Chicago, IL, 800-397-2282, www.actapublications.com.

Library of Congress Catalog number: 2022933229

Hardcover ISBN: 978-0-87946-703-6
Paperback ISBN: 978-0-87946-717-3
Printed in the United States of America by Total Printing Systems
Year 30 29 28 27 26 25 24 23 22
Printing 10 9 8 7 6 5 4 3 2 First

Text printed on 30% post-consumer recycled paper

Contents

Dedication

For My Beautiful Wife, Miran Lee

The Merton Prayer

My Lord God,
I have no idea where I am going.
I do not see the road ahead of me.
I cannot know for certain where it will end.
Nor do I really know myself,
and the fact that I think that I am following your will
does not mean that I am actually doing so.

But I believe that the desire to please you
does in fact please you.
And I hope I have that desire in all that I am doing.
I hope that I will never do anything apart from that desire.
And I know that if I do this you will lead me by the right road,
though I may know nothing about it.

Therefore, I will trust you always,
though I may seem to be lost and in the shadow of death.

I will not fear,
for you are ever with me,
and you will never leave me to face my perils alone.[1]

---

1. Thomas Merton, *Thoughts in Solitude* (Farrar, Straus, Giroux Publishing, 1956, 1958, 2009) p. 79. Used with permission.

Introduction

My opposing counsel surprised me by asking if I wanted to ride back with him to my downtown Chicago law office. We had chatted amicably at a couple of other depositions but had never spoken socially outside of the courtroom or deposition room.

The reason for his unexpected request became apparent quickly enough. "Steven, I noticed in your briefcase a book by Thomas Merton. Are you by chance aware of his 'I don't know where I'm going' prayer?" Then, in a way that communicated rare and authentic vulnerability, he said, "This prayer has saved my life, over and over. It has gotten me through a divorce, drug addiction, suicidal thoughts, deaths of loved ones, and career ending mistakes. I could not have survived without this prayer in my life."

I told him, "Yes, I know The Merton Prayer well; it has also been a huge part of my ongoing connection with God." That lawyer and I became friends and have shared many other encounters about our Christian journeys, but there has never been another conversation I have had with anyone about anything that has changed my life like this one did.

I believe that conversation, in 2014, gave birth to the ideas for this book. The Merton Prayer, which has meant so much to me, has obviously helped countless others in their walk with God. This is a book for all Christ-followers, of any and all "flavors of Christendom,"[2] and I have no theological bones to pick with anyone in these pages, so please proceed knowing that the only goal is to share my thoughts on this life-changing and life-enhancing prayer, known worldwide as "The Merton Prayer."

When I first read this prayer, it was as if I had come home to a place where I met God and God met me. It felt like an old comfortable quilt made by my grandma, which a child could cuddle in on rainy cold days in front of a crackling fire—perhaps while drinking hot chocolate. It also felt like a magnet that drew me to God and would not let me go. No matter what my circumstances of life were at the time, this prayer gave me strength, which in turn led to real peace and filled me with confidence that God was *"ever with me"* and indeed would *"never leave me to face my perils alone."*

So how did a Protestant-Evangelical-Christian, former clergyman-turned-trial-attorney in Chicago, ever find "I don't know where I'm going," a prayer written by a famous yet seemingly unapproachable (to me) Catholic Trappist monk from Kentucky? How did it become my own immersive exercise in authenticity?

---

2. I have given seminar presentations on The Merton Prayer to the Thomas Merton Society's Chicago Chapter and the Christian Legal Society's National Conference; both audiences responded with great interest in the words of this prayer.

It is from Merton's book *Thoughts in Solitude*,[3] and I confess that when I got to that one-page prayer in 1990, I stopped reading, and honestly, do not believe that I have ever read the remainder of that book, though I have devoured many other books written by Merton. I simply could not and cannot get past the prayer.

Since that first encounter, the words of The Merton Prayer have been with me every single day. I soon came to have it memorized and realized that I could not go through a day without meditating on it. I say it to myself on my way to work; I say it out loud in the health club steam room (if nobody else is present!); I talk about it so often in my small accountability men's group that the others often say, "Look out, here comes Merton again!" I pray the prayer at the beginning of my daily "quiet time;" phrases from it end up attached to my "breath prayers" (short prayers uttered with inhalation and exhalation) as I walk to and from courtrooms. A copy is posted by my computer in my office. The Merton Prayer quickly became an integral part of my inner being.

But never, in my wildest dreams, did I ever think that it would save my life. But it did. And that is what this book is about.

Scripture, from the Gospels, a Psalm, Paul's words, or one of Solomon's proverbs, constantly spring out to me and often elucidate and confirm phrases from The Merton Prayer. My seminary Professor of Hebrew, John Ralls, told a story of a Talmudic rabbi whose students asked him, "Rabbi, how best does one study Torah?" The rabbi responded, "Turn it, turn it, turn it. It's all there."

---

3. Thomas Merton, *Thoughts in Solitude* (Farrar, Straus, Giroux Publishing, 1956, 1958, 2009) p. 79.

That's how I feel about Merton's prayer. Alongside the "Lord's Prayer"[4] taught to us by Jesus himself, the "Serenity Prayer,"[5] attributed to or at least made possible by Protestant theologian Reinhold Niebuhr, which is the guiding prayer for so many struggling with addictions, and the Old Testament "Prayer of Jabez,"[6] I believe that The Merton Prayer can be a model prayer for Christians seeking greater authenticity in their prayer life. The 158 words of this amazing prayer may become for you, as they have for me and many others, a powerful connector to God. I encourage you to pray The Merton Prayer every day, as you turn to God with your petitions, thanks, and intentions.

My goal in Part One of this book is to introduce you to Thomas Merton, the author of this amazing prayer. Then, in Part Two, we will dig deeply into the words of the prayer and "Turn it, turn it, turn it" because, indeed as the rabbi said, "it's all there." Merton's words live on for new generations of God-seekers. Finally, in the

---

4. Matthew 6:9-13; Luke 11:2-4; also known as "The Our Father."

5. "God grant me the serenity to accept the things I cannot change, courage to change the things I can, and wisdom to know the difference." Often attributed to American theologian Reinhold Niebuhr. See https://en.wikipedia.org/wiki/Serenity_Prayer.

6. The Prayer of Jabez is found in I Chronicles 4:10: "Oh that you would bless me and expand my territory! Please be with me in all that I do and keep me from all trouble and pain!" See John W. Mauck, *The Healing of Jabez* (Credo House Publishers, 2009); and Bruce Wilkenson, *The Prayer of Jabez: Breaking Through to the Blessed Life* (Multnomah, 2000).

Appendices, I will share more of my own background and experience for readers who are interested. But you are welcome to skip that part (as my publisher constantly reminds me that the point of this book is Thomas Merton, his prayer, and how it might change your life as it has changed mine).

Steven A. Denny
Oak Park, Illinois
Easter 2022

PART ONE

Why The Merton Prayer ... and Why Merton?

One of my mentors in Merton, Sr. Suzanne Zuercher, OSB, made a clever and true distinction between the "prayer" and the "pray-er"[7]: one word, two very different concepts, she'd say. One word is the content of the action; the other is the actor who creates the content. The two words are interwoven, to be sure, and should The Merton Prayer become part of your own psyche, as it has mine, you will become a different pray-er. You will become one who comfortably practices Brother Lawrence's "presence of God," even when you, like Lawrence, are picking up the raisins you have dropped all over the kitchen floor![8]

Why dig into The Merton Prayer? The simple answer is that this prayer has captivated Christians ever since it was first published, and believers world-wide have repeated and memorized this prayer as part of their daily spiritual journey. It brings comfort and guidance, sets the plate for real surrender, and quickly gets a person's perspective back on what is–and what is not–truly important in life.

So many books have been written about Thomas Merton[9] it would be a disservice should I attempt here anything other than

7. Suzanne Zuercher, *Using the Enneagram in Prayer* (Ave Maria Press, 2008) p. 2.

8. Brother Lawrence, *The Practice of the Presence of God* (ICS Publications, 1994).

9. I highly recommend the amazing PBS documentary by Morgan C. Atkinson, *Soul Searching: The Journey of Thomas Merton* (Public Broadcasting System, 2007). It is also a book by the same title (Liturgical Press, 2008).

a cursory biographical sketch.[10] Filmmaker and author Morgan Atkinson reports being asked by Lawrence Cunningham of Notre Dame: "What Thomas Merton are you interested in? ... Are you interested in Thomas Merton the monk? Are you interested in Thomas Merton the literary critic? Are you interested in Thomas Merton the poet? The social justice person? The person of peace? The guy who writes on spiritual theology? There are many Thomas Mertons, at least from the perspective of his writings."[11]

One of my other favorite "spiritual formation" authors, the Franciscan priest Richard Rohr, was significantly influenced by the writings of Thomas Merton. I agree wholeheartedly with his succinct analysis: "I believe Thomas Merton is probably the most significant American Catholic of the twentieth century, along with

---

10. Popular biographies of Thomas Merton: *Thomas Merton: An Introduction to His Life, Teachings, and Practices* by Jon M. Sweeney (St. Martin's Essentials, 2021); *The Seven Mountains of Thomas Merton* by Michael Mott (Harcourt Brace, 1984); and *Merton: A Biography* by Monica Furlong (Liguori Publications, 1980). Also I highly recommend: *Encounters with Merton* by Henri Nouwen (Crossroad Publishing, 1972); *Merton's Palace of Nowhere* by James Finley [who was a novice at Gethsemani under Merton] (Ave Maria Press, 1978); *Heretic Blood: The Spiritual Geography of Thomas Merton* by Michael Higgins (Stoddart Publishing, 1998); *Thomas Merton: The Courage for Truth; Letters to Writers* (Farrar, Straus, Giroux, 1993); and [one of the most enjoyable, unusual, and fun books I have ever read] *The Monk's Record Player: Thomas Merton, Bob Dylan, and the Perilous Summer of 1966* by Robert Hudson (Eerdmans Publishing, 2018).

11. Morgan Atkinson and Jonathan Montaldo, editors, *Soul Searching: The Journey of Thomas Merton* (Liturgical Press, 2008) pp. 8-9.

Dorothy Day. His whole life is a parable and a paradox, like all of ours; but he had an uncanny ability to describe his inner life with God for the rest of us."[12] I would alter Rohr's words "American Catholic" to "American Christian" or even "American spiritual thinker" since Merton has crossed denominational and even interfaith lines like few others I have encountered.

When Pope Francis addressed the United States Congress in 2015, he caused a research frenzy of sorts among news organizations. The Pope lauded four Americans—Abraham Lincoln, Martin Luther King, Dorothy Day, and Thomas Merton—as people who had "made America a better place because of their dreams of justice, equal rights, liberty, and peace." The reference to Merton by the Pope led to numerous articles in the press that explained to a curious American public just who this Merton person was.[13]

Here is a very brief overview of Thomas Merton's life: [14]

---

12. Richard Rohr, *Falling Upward: A Spirituality for the Two Halves of Life* (Jossey-Bass, 2011) pp. 161-162.

13. For example, see the NPR article written by Bill Chappell titled "In Pope Francis' Congress Speech, Praise for Dorothy Day and Thomas Merton" (National Public Radio, September 24, 2015), https://www.npr.org/sections/the two-way/2015/09/24/ 443126027/in-pope-francis-congress-speech-praise-for-dorothy-day-and-thomas-merton

14. For a quick presentation of the facts of his life see: "Thomas Merton," *Encyclopedia Britannica*, February 21, 2020, https://www.britannica.com/biography/Thomas-Merton; and George Kilcourse, "Merton Overview," Bellarmine University, 2019, https://www. bellarmine.edu/merton-centennial/overview/

- Thomas Merton was born in 1915 in Prades, France.
- His American-born mother, Ruth Jenkins, died in 1921 when Thomas was only six.
- His New Zealand-born artist father, Owen Merton, died in 1931 when Thomas was only sixteen.
- He was a student at three different boarding schools, in France and England.
- In 1933, he attended Cambridge University where he majored in French and Italian.
- In 1934, he left Cambridge and moved to America.
- In 1935, he enrolled at Columbia University in New York.
- At Columbia, he became the editor of the *1937 Yearbook* as well as Art Editor of the *Columbia Jester.*
- He graduated in 1938 and began work on a master's degree.
- On November 16, 1938, he was baptized and received into the Catholic Church at Corpus Christi in New York City.
- He taught English at St. Bonaventure College in 1940-41.
- On December 10, 1941, he entered the Trappist Monastery south of Bardstown, Kentucky, known as The Abbey of Our Lady of Gethsemani.[15]

---

15. The fact that Merton showed up at the gates of Gethsemani only three days after the Japanese bombed Pearl Harbor and America was thrust into World War II, is certainly a source of speculation by many. See: Marie Theresa Coombs, *Mystery Hidden Yet Revealed* (Cascade Books, 2003); James Thomas Baker, *Thomas Merton Social Critic* (University of Kentucky, 1971, 2009); and Andrew Lenoir, "What Would Thomas Merton Make of Trump, Climate Change and Twitter?," in *America: The Jesuit Review*, October 3, 2017.

- Merton wrote over 70 books about spiritual life, including journals and poetry.[16]
- He taught the novice monks at the monastery.
- For many years he lived alone in a hermitage on the Abbey's grounds.
- He died in 1968, on December 10th, the exact same day of the year on which he had entered Gethsemani, twenty-seven years earlier.

The official name of the order Merton joined, commonly known as Trappists, is the Order of Cistercians of the Strict Observance (originally named the Order of Reformed Cistercians of Our Lady of La Trappe), among the most austere orders that follow the Rule of St. Benedict. All Trappist communities are dedicated to silence and contemplation. Monks learn sign language to communicate while working during the day. The motto at a Trappist monastery is *ora et labora* (pray and work), which basically covered the everyday life of Merton and his fellow monks when he was alive and at Gethsemani.

The Liturgy of the Hours in monastic life involves eight different times of formal prayer in the sanctuary, beginning at 3:15 am

---

16. My favorite books by Merton, in order: *The Seven Storey Mountain* (Harcourt Brace Jovanovich, Publishers, 1948); *The Sign of Jonas* (Harcourt Brace Jovanovich, Publishers, 1953); *The Asian Journal of Thomas Merton* (New Directions Publishing Corporation, 1968); and *Zen and the Birds of Appetite* (New Directions Publishing Corporation, 1968).

with Vigils and concluding at 7:30 pm with Compline.[17] The entire corpus of the Psalms is sung/chanted antiphonally by the monks every two weeks.[18] From my experience of being in the Gethsemani balcony observing the monks at worship, it is clear to me that all 150 of the Psalms are memorized by many of the monks, who sing the Psalms without even looking at the music in front of them.

As Merton rode the train to Kentucky in 1941, he hoped he would be accepted into the monastery at Gethsemani, a hope tempered by the reality of the looming World War II and the very real possibility that he might be drafted into the military.

> Mile after mile my desire to be in the monastery increased beyond belief. I was altogether absorbed in that one idea. And yet, paradoxically mile after mile my indifference increased, and my interior peace. What if they did not receive me? Then I would go to the army. But surely that would be a disaster? Not at all. If, after all this, I was rejected by the monastery and had to be drafted, it would be quite clear that it was God's will. I had done everything that was in my power; the rest was in His hands. And for all the tremendous and increasing intensity of my desire to be in the cloister, the thought that I

---

17. At Gethsemani the daily schedule of prayers are Vigils (3:15 am), Lauds (5:45 am), Eucharist (6:15 am), Terce (7:30 am), Sext (12:15 pm), None (2:15 pm), Vespers (5:30 pm), and Compline (7:30 pm).

18. Antiphonal singing or chanting is when a group is divided into two groups facing each other and the groups alternate with each phrase of the Psalm.

might find myself, instead, in an army camp no longer troubled me in the least.[19]

To me, the above quote from the very young monk, published in his seventh year at Gethsemani, confirms that he was then already living the precepts of The Merton Prayer, knowing that the Lord was "leading him on the right road" though that was not at all clear to him as the train lumbered toward the monastery. The Merton Prayer, first published in 1958, was likely created by Merton during his early years at the monastery, in the mid-1940s, during his well-known search for more solitude. Indeed, The Merton Prayer may have been first written down by him while praying in St. Anne's, a tiny chapel-hut at Gethsemane (described and pictured in the Appendix).

The gate at Gethsemani, which reads in bold permanent print "GOD ALONE," was indeed opened to Merton, and he lived there for the next twenty-seven years. It absolutely boggles my mind to think what the world might have missed had his "road" taken him into the military and not the cloister at Gethsemani.

In 1968, after lecturing to Buddhist monks in Thailand, Merton was accidentally electrocuted by a fan that fell into his bathtub as he showered. His body was returned to the U.S. on a transport plane that was carrying many American soldiers who had been killed in Viet Nam (the irony of which is ripe and often noted, given Merton's anti-war writings). He was buried in the Gethsemani cemetery with a white cross which says simply "Father

19. Thomas Merton, *The Seven Storey Mountain* (Harcourt, Inc., 1948, 1996, 1998) p. 406.

Louis."[20] I have been told, and have not confirmed, that his body may be the only embalmed body buried at Gethsemani, and one of only two bodies buried in a casket.

Byron Borger, a brilliant bookstore owner from Pennsylvania,[21] who has an amazingly vast knowledge of Christian authors, shared with me the following encounter he had with a man who went to school with "Tom" at Columbia. To Byron's question, "What was Merton like in college?" the man said simply, "I heard he put himself into a monastery and I never heard from him since, but I guess he wrote a lot of books!" Indeed, Thomas Merton wrote "a lot of books," one of which is *Thoughts in Solitude* from which comes "The Merton Prayer."[22]

Ronnie McBrayer, a pastor-author, after noting what a prolific author Merton was, commented, "If he did nothing else than pen what is now called 'The Merton Prayer,' he did enough. Honest and searching, it is Merton at his best and, if you are like me, you will find yourself returning to it time and again."[23]

Let's unpack The Merton Prayer together and see where it leads us.

---

20. Every monk is given a new name upon entry into Gethsemani. Merton's was "Louis."

21. Hearts and Minds Books (bookstore), Dallastown, Pennsylvania.

22. Thomas Merton, *Thoughts in Solitude* (Farrar, Straus, Giroux Publishing, 1956, 1958, 2009) p.79.

23. Ronnie McBrayer, "You Will Find Honest Truth in 'The Merton Prayer,'" *The Detroit News*, December 7, 2019, https://www.detroitnews.com/story/life/advice/2019/12/07/ronnie-mcbrayer-merton-prayer/40774201/.

PART TWO

Unpacking The Merton Prayer

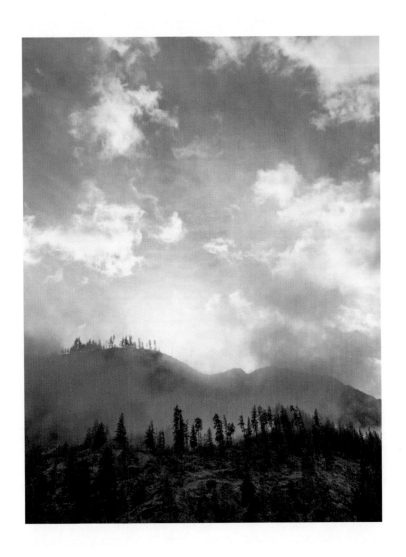

A NOTE TO THE READER

There are fourteen sections in Part Two: Unpacking The Merton Prayer. Each section addresses a phrase or sentence of the 158 words that make up The Merton Prayer. There are five parts to each section.

Visual Metaphor

An original photograph by my friend Dr. Stephen L. Hufman[1] introduces each chapter. The photographs give you an opportunity to reflect on any initial reactions and responses that might be evoked by the few words of The Merton Prayer explored in that chapter.

Scriptural Bases

This section is by no means intended to be exhaustive, and you are invited to enjoy the passages I have accumulated while keeping an eye out for your own "catchings" of Merton's prayer phrases in other passages of the Bible. Indeed, as this prayer becomes part of your daily walk with God you will likely be amazed, as I was and am still, to see just how often a scriptural passage jumps out at

1. For more amazing photography by Stephen L. Hufman, M.D., along with his powerful devotional thoughts, see his site www.Stephen-Hufman.com.

you with confirmation of exactly what Merton said in his prayer. (Scripture passages are from the *New Living Translation* unless otherwise noted.)

Exegesis

This is a very familiar word to those who preach and teach scripture; it is literally the "leading out" of the meaning, from two Greek words: *ek* "out of, from" and *ago* "to go, to lead." Hence, when one "exegetes" scripture, one "leads out" of the words the meaning of the words. For example, when I tell you that a Greek imperative is in the present tense, it is "exegesis" that allows me to share with you that Jesus didn't just say "Ask, Seek, and Knock." The real meaning of his words is that we are to "ask and *keep on asking, making our asking a matter of daily habitual behavior.*"

Or this example: the famous exchange between Jesus and Peter in John 21:15. Jesus asks Peter, "Do you love me with *agape* (unconditional love) more than these?" Peter, "Yes, Lord I love you with *phileo* (brotherly love)." Jesus (again), "Do you love me with *agape* love?" Peter (again), "Yes, Lord I love you with *phileo* love." Jesus, having tried twice but not getting a response, then changes his question, "Do you love me with *phileo* love?" Peter, "[Duh, I've told you this twice already!] Yes, Lord I love you with *phileo* love!"

In a court of law, an objection would immediately be made as follows: "Judge, Peter's first two answers are *non-responsive* and should be stricken." Peter then would be told by the Judge, "Answer the question which is asked!"

The above are two examples of exegesis. They "lead out" the meaning from the words of the text. So, with the words of The Merton Prayer, I will attempt to go deeper and provide a starting place for you to get into the real meaning that God might have for you from this prayer.

Personal Stories

It is in this section where I will get personal and share with you how God has met me through The Merton Prayer on my daily walks, in the conundrums of my life, in my disappointments, in my joys, in my life-threatening brush with death, and in my unexpected career change. I will at times share some "journeys" from spiritual companions, family, and close friends, whom God has brought into my life. I will also point to real-life situations I have read or heard about that bring Merton's words alive.

My goal in this section is again to nudge you toward seeing similar times and events in your own life where—now in hindsight and tomorrow in foresight—you might see God's hand actually on your shoulder. That famous photo of two walking on a beach where only one set of footprints is seen and the explanation—"well, that's when Jesus was carrying you"–will, I hope, become real for you, as it so very much has become real for me!

Turn It, Turn It, Turn It

Finally, I try to stimulate serious and deep reflection on the words of the chapter's phrase of The Merton Prayer. These questions and suggested topics are my attempt to be helpful to an individual or a small group intent on deepening their walk with God.

My final suggestion is that you recite the prayer in its entirety each time you pick up this book. I had a housemate in college who would nightly stand in the doorway of my room and tell me the five important things he had learned in class that day; he was repeating this in order to reinforce the content and drive it deeper into his consciousness. Repetition helps with familiarity, which helps bring comfort, all of which will help the words of The Merton Prayer become very natural for you.

Let's now dig into this prayer and "turn it, turn it, turn it" because indeed, it's all there–what God wants you to find and what will breathe life into your spirit.

My prayer for you: Lord God, friend of Thomas Merton, please bless every searcher who deigns to explore this great prayer with him and me.

I

"My Lord God"

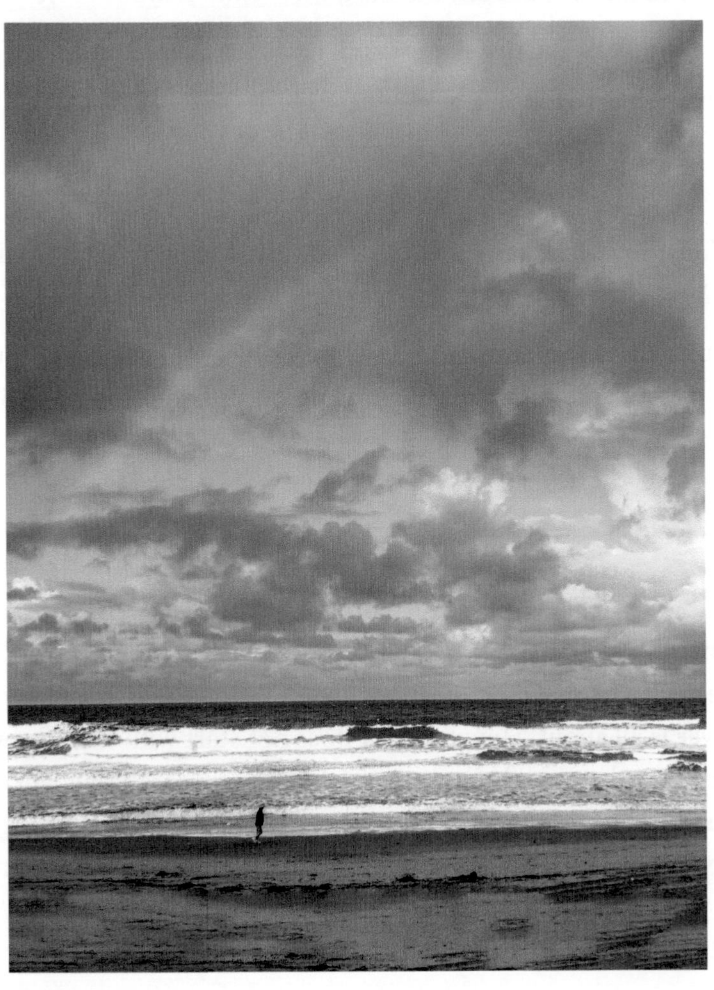

Scriptural Bases

O God, you are my God. Psalm 63:1

Then I will live among the people of Israel and be their God, and they will know that I am the Lord their God. Exodus 29:45-46

They will call on my name, and I will answer them. I will say, "These are my people," and they will say, "The Lord is our God." Zechariah 13:9

The LORD is my shepherd. Psalm 23:1

O Lord my God, my Holy One, you who are eternal. Habakkuk 1:12a

"I have been the Lord your God ever since I brought you out of Egypt. You must acknowledge no God but me, for there is no other savior." Hosea 13:4

Exegesis

My is a first-person possessive pronoun that always connotes ownership. "*My* Lord God." Really? Can we ever "own" the Lord God? The very personal relationship with the Lord God is what Merton's prayer is all about. How fitting it does not start with the prayer cliché we in the church (and many of us in our correspondence use most often: "Dear....") To me, this very first word of The Merton Prayer—*My*—shocks me at a deep level, starts me on the connecting path of knowing who I am, who I am not, and who God is. "You and I, God, we've got this thing going on between us which is *so very* personal and real that I have permission to claim ownership and address you as 'My,' all the while knowing that you are 'My' to so many others all the time and at the same time!" The agony of Psalm 22 begins with the same words from David, repeated with the same sense of awe by Jesus on the cross: "*My* God, *my* God."[2]

"Lord" is the Greek word *kurios* which also has a meaning of "master" or "owner." This second word of Merton's prayer calms my need to be loved and wanted, since God *owns* me! God is my master, owner, Lord over my every breath. I am only two words into this prayer and have enough to chew on for hours: "I know *whose* I am. Freely and lovingly I am *God's*!"

"God," of course, is a super-rich word for Christians, which conjures up such depth I could get lost in a monster Bible study right now. Behind the Greek *theos* (God) is the Hebrew *tetragrammaton* (Greek meaning "four letters"), the four Hebrew letters of the ineffable and unspeakable name of God, that is, YHWH. The rabbis had such great respect for the name of God that they refused to say it out loud and even replaced the vowel points from the more general word for God, *adonai*, onto those four letters YHWH. In reading the text the rabbis, when encountering the letters *YHWH* would pronounce the word as if it had the vowels of *adonai*. Hence, we have our pronunciation "Yahweh," which when anglicized has often been rendered "Jehovah." Many English translations of the Bible will capitalize all four

2. Jesus speaking the Hebrew "*Eli Eli*" was mistakenly thought by the people who heard him at the time to be calling for the prophet Elijah. See Matthew 27:46 and also Mark 15:34 (*Eloi Eloi*).

letters of the word *LORD* as an unstated homage to the Hebrew *tetragrammaton*.

Moses asks God in Exodus 3:13, "What is your name?" and the cryptic response from God is difficult to translate: "I Am who I Am" is the usual translation. However, the verb *Am* is just as likely a *hiphil* (a Hebrew verb with causative mood rather than indicative mood), and its meaning would connote something more like, "I cause to be what I cause to be!" A simple future tense translation is also available, "I will be what I will be." The Creator God who set the stars in the heavens, that's "Who" sends you, Moses, and this same almighty God is the One I am crying out to when I say the first three words of The Merton Prayer.

So, we have begun this prayer with three simple words establishing who I am, whose I am, and who I am not. What a powerful beginning, worthy of much contemplation along with great joy. And, of course, the first of the many Psalm 23 scriptural bases for The Merton Prayer could not be clearer: The LORD is *my* shepherd; that is, the Creator God who flung the stars into the universe is *my* personal Shepherd. And what do shepherds do? They protect and lead their flocks!

Personal Stories

For thirty-three years, I daily walked on the downtown Chicago streets in the area known as The Loop. I often would try to offset the stress of the concrete jungle by seeking respite in a wonderful, beautiful church a block from my office. St. Peter's Catholic Church has Masses several times on weekdays, and in the time between the Masses people come to sit in contemplative meditation and prayer.

St. Peter's became my "go to place" for peace and quiet, to reconnect with God. The fifth row on the right side down front was my "sacred pew." Why? About fifteen feet in front of me was a wonderful statue that brought me such incredible comfort and inner joy. Jesus, my Lord and Savior, is holding a small child, or so I thought. (Every Catholic reading this now will undoubtedly know where this story is going.)

A couple of years ago, when my wife, Miran, accompanied me to St. Peter's for Mass, I was excited to show her the sacred spot which had helped me *for decades* feel that my Lord and Savior Jesus was holding me tightly, just as Jesus was holding that little child. I had put myself in the child's place so many times and had always left that sanctuary renewed in my love for my Savior and his love for me. Miran very gently leaned close to my ear, "Sweetheart, that is not Jesus holding a child; that is Joseph holding Jesus." (I beg the reader for a little grace here, since I am a Protestant after all, and we Protestants just never got to learn much about statues in church.)

Immediately my heart was flooded with fond loving memories of how my own earthly father had held me tenderly as a child. When I was three or four years old, I would lie down in the second church pew on the right side in the Broadway Christian Church in Lexington, Kentucky—my little feet in my mother's lap and my head on my father's knee. Daddy would gently stroke my hair and pat my head all through the worship service. I never felt so loved in all my life, and this marble statue at St. Peter's had resurrected those incredible feelings for decades, without my even knowing *who* was actually holding *whom*.

I was eight years old when I had walked down the aisle of my home chuch and made my "profession of faith." I repeated these words as our minister led me along each phrase: "I believe that Jesus is the Christ, the son of the living God, and I accept him as my personal Lord and Savior." The words of my profession of faith mirror the first three words of The Merton Prayer: "My Lord God." I had stated before the whole world that Jesus was the Christ, the Son of the Living God, and that he was my "personal Lord and Savior."

Following my confession of faith, I went to a changing room where I donned a white robe to experience what Protestants call the "believer's baptism."[3] Once clothed in my robe, I went to a spot near the baptistry where there was a young girl, one of my Sunday School friends, who had also made her profession of faith that morning; she was being baptized before me (girls first, don't you know). We both huddled and shivered a bit as we stood near the baptistry steps, while the pastor walked down into the water. My friend went first, and I watched her walk down the three or four steps into the water.

Now here is where my memory, perchance, may get a tad conflated with what is and what is not reality. I was wearing my

3. As with many Protestant Churches, "believer's baptism" in my home congregation was available to adults and children who could articulate their own statement of faith; it was done by "immersion," in a tank (baptistry) filled with water deep enough for the pastor to dunk the candidate fully under the water.

usual “tighty-whitey” underpants beneath my baptismal robe, so I assumed that my Sunday School classmate was clothed likewise beneath her robe. Much to my eight-year-old surprise, once she entered the baptistry waters I saw that she had on blue underpants. I often wonder if that vision might in any way have invalidated my baptism’s effectiveness. (Perhaps Dr. Jung or Dr. Freud might weigh in on any significant psychological damage the “blue underwear image” from my eight-year-old psyche may have wrought in my adult life.)

Once I was in the water and the pastor proclaimed that I was “being obedient to my Lord in Christian baptism,” I knew that indeed I “was being raised up out of the water to walk in the newness of life in Christ Jesus.” Having baptized by immersion many new Christ-followers in my career as a pastor, I have never lost that amazing feeling of “walking in the newness of life” with one’s personal Lord and Savior.

Call me simple-minded, call me an eternal optimist, call me a child whose parents loved him and who felt the pull of the Holy Spirit in my little heart. Whatever you think, this I know for certain—from that day until now, Jesus Christ has been “My Lord God” and my life has had a purpose and meaning. Many of the roads I took had twists and turns, some leading to great successes and others resulting in spectacular failures. There were some short seasons where God and I were barely on speaking terms, a tad estranged from one another, so to speak, but the pull of that child-like faith has never left me. You will hear about some of these roads I traveled as you journey with me though The Merton Prayer.

If you were to ask any of my three children what they remember about my waking them up on Easter morning when they were very young, I hope they would recall my rousing them with these words, "Jesus is alive! He has risen from the grave! Because he lives, we have purpose for our lives and a meaning to our existence." The apostle Paul said, "And if Christ has not been raised, then all our preaching is useless, and your faith is useless" (I Corinthians 15:14). Rarely do I prefer the King James translations, but here is one place I do: "then is our preaching vain, and your faith is also vain."

"Useless" and "vain" describe my life without a risen Savior. When I say those words "My Lord God" at the beginning of this prayer, my universe is ordered, my purpose for life is clear, my existence as a human being makes sense. If the Bible is simply a collection of old myths, if there is no Creator-God, if Jesus was just a teacher whose body was stolen by followers perpetrating the biggest fraud in history, then "useless" and "vain" would have been my Hallmark-calling-card attempt to rouse my children.

Someone once told me that the likelihood of our world coming into existence without an intelligent designer at its origin (for Christians read, Yahweh, the Creator God of the Bible) is tantamount to believing that the unabridged twenty-volume Oxford English Dictionary (OED) came into existence from an explosion in a type-setting factory. In my opinion, it takes more "faith" to believe the OED just "happened" than it does to believe that the world, the human body, the complexity of the human eye, the balance in nature, etc., etc., etc., were created by My Lord God—the intelligent designer and all-powerful Creator.

I happily and loudly and daily proclaim, "My Lord God," over and over. Psalm Eight[4] and the hymn "How Great Thou Art"[5] both come to my consciousness when I pray The Merton Prayer's first three words. Thank you, Thomas Merton, for orienting me to my purpose for existing with the words "My Lord God," and thank you, My Lord God, for leading me to share this man's prayer.

Turn It, Turn It, Turn It

1. What feels comfortable or uncomfortable to you about starting a prayer with "My Lord God?" What does it mean to your walk with God if you view the Creator of the Universe as "yours?" Do these first three words help you feel closer to God? Why or why not?

2. My prayer life before The Merton Prayer usually found me beginning with "Dear Heavenly Father" or something very

4. "O Lord, our Lord, your majestic name fills the earth! ... When I look at the night sky and see the work of your fingers—the moon and the stars you set in place—what are mere mortals that you should think about them, human beings that you should care for them?" (Psalm 8:1a, 3-4)

5. "O Lord my God/when I in awesome wonder/consider all the worlds thy hands have made/I see the stars, I hear the rolling thunder/ Thy power throughout the universe displayed/Then sings my soul, my Savior God to Thee/how great Thou art/how great Thou art." From *How Great Thou Art* (hymn), based on a poem by Carl Boberg, *O Great God,* 1885.

similar. This opening three-word phrase of The Merton Prayer—"My Lord God"—boldly claims a much deeper and personal relationship between the pray-er and God. Try beginning a prayer this way and make note of how it feels to you.

3. Reflect on a time when you cried out to God. What precipitated that prayer? How did God respond? How has that experience changed you?

4. How does the paradox of dual ownership in this phrase (God owns me and I own God) both comfort and challenge you in your current situation?

5. Psalm 91:2 affirms that "God alone is my refuge." Have you been relying on a different "god," something else that dominates your emotions, thoughts, and actions (perhaps another person, a job title/position, or even an illness or a difficult painful memory)? What might it mean to switch allegiances and focus to the God of the Psalmist and of The Merton Prayer?

II

"I Have No Idea Where I Am Going"

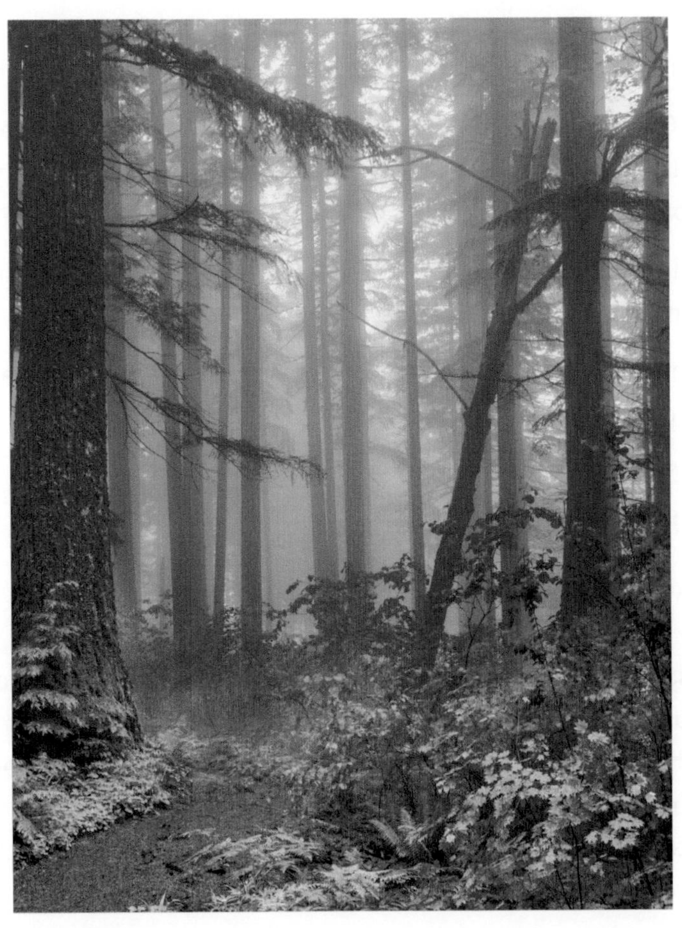

Scriptural Bases

Your road led through the sea, your pathway through the mighty waters—a pathway no one knew was there! Psalm 77:19

I pondered the direction of my life, and I turned to follow your laws. Psalm 119:59

Show me where to walk, for I give myself to you.... May your gracious Spirit lead me forward on a firm footing. Psalm 143:8b, 10b

Our God...we have no power to face this vast army that is attacking us. We do not know what to do, but our eyes are on you. 2 Chronicles 20:12 (NIV)

I will lead blind Israel down a new path, guiding them along an unfamiliar way. Isaiah 42:16

I know, Lord, that our lives are not our own. We are not able to plan our own course. Jeremiah 10:23

Exegesis

The words *I have* state a fact (known grammatically as the indicative mood), which always affirms that the reality of the verb's message is not open to discussion. It connotes that something actually and really has happened—with zero chance of it *not* being true. Other grammatical moods point the action to a "probability," "remote possibility," or even "hardly likely." This phrase of The Merton Prayer means "without a doubt or any question, I actually, and really, have zero idea where I am going right now!"

On the other hand, the word *idea* can be as broad as possible, connoting a "hint," a "suggestion," a "likelihood," or even a "10% chance." So, Merton's juxtaposition of the solid, unequivocal phrase *I have* with the loose words *no idea* is devastatingly unclear and surprisingly honest.

Seriously? Come on now, Thomas! Surely you have a "hint" of where you are going. At least you know in which compass direction. Not even north, south, east, or west? (Or perhaps you are like my friend Linda Vander Naald, a public-school paraprofessional with first-graders, who admits that she never knows for sure what direction on the compass she is headed. If so, then this phrase is easy for you to experience.)

I choose to take the certainty of the ambiguity of this phrase literally, and it just knocks me up-side-of-the-head with a two-by-four (one of many Kentuckyisms likely to appear in this book).

In my not-so-humble opinion, with this phrase Merton is not referencing his eternal destination options—i.e., heaven and hell. Indeed, the entire context of The Merton Prayer speaks of multiple roads in *this* life, roads often leading in starkly opposite directions. Each of us praying Merton's prayer must make decisions as to which roads we must follow and which we must avoid. Our final destination is simply not addressed here.

Personal Stories

"Mr. Denny, I will give you five minutes to answer the defendant's motion for a directed verdict against your client." It was 11:00 pm on a Thursday night in August 2007 on the twenty-fourth floor of the Cook County Courthouse in downtown Chicago. For two weeks I had presented my case to a jury on behalf of a 34-year-old-widow with an 18-month-old son whose husband/father had died following his doctor's awful failure to diagnose and treat Acute Lymphoblastic Leukemia, perhaps the most curable of all leukemias. Incredibly, the doctor never had done a blood test or taken a chest x-ray, even though his nurse's note indicated that the man had been coughing up "red phlegm" (which means the presence of blood and not, as the doctor amazingly tried to convince the jury, simply red cough drops).

All of my expert witnesses had testified well, my client had done a great job, and I felt good about my cross-examination of the defendant doctor's expert witnesses. The next day, Friday, was to be closing arguments, where each side gets to tell the jury what they believe the evidence has shown and to ask for a verdict in favor of their side.

To say I was exhausted might be the greatest understatement ever made by a human being. I was a sole practitioner, which means that in my office I was the only lawyer. The doctor had hired one of the largest law firms in the country, and there were three opposing attorneys working full-time on this case.

So, as midnight approached, I and one of the defense team attorneys were finishing up from a very long day with rulings on jury instructions, while the other two attorneys working for the defense were either home sleeping or working on their closing arguments which would start at 9:00 a.m. the next morning. I believe I had not eaten anything since lunch and I was slightly dehydrated, needing water. At the conclusion of the judge's rulings on jury instructions, the defense attorney surprised me by handing the judge a Motion for Directed Verdict. This motion, if granted, would effectively end the case in favor of the doctor.[6] The trial would be over; there would be no closing arguments; and in the morning the jury would be thanked and sent home.

"Mr. Denny, it's very late, so you must give me your response to this motion right now!" The judge's words were ringing in my ears. I recall that my knees were shaking, and I felt the need to sit down. "Your Honor, may I please leave the courtroom for five minutes and then return with my answer?" The judge graciously granted my request.

I walked out of the courtroom and went to the bank of floor-to-ceiling windows which looked south over the Chicago Loop. I stood at the window and realized that I was fixating on one object in the skyline, which was just across the street from the courthouse. The First United Methodist Church, also more popularly known as the Chicago Temple, has a small chapel nestled in the tower of the building at 77 W. Washington, far above the street and its beautiful sanctuary below on the ground floor. Tourists from all over the world visit this "Chapel in the Sky," as it is popularly called, and I had been there often myself.

As I stood at that window, staring at this place of worship, which was almost at eye-level with the twenty-fourth floor of the

---

6. This Motion for Directed Verdict essentially said to the judge, "Now that Mr. Denny has presented his entire case, you judge have to dismiss this case as a matter of law since he hasn't successfully proved that the doctor did anything wrong."

courthouse, I repeated softly out loud the words of The Merton Prayer. I literally had "no idea" how to respond to this motion. Not a clue. Not a hint. My mind was racing since I could frame two opposing responses, and I just simply could not decide which one would be the correct answer for my client.

I knew the law around directed verdict motions well, and I knew that my client's case would be lost if I gave the judge the wrong reason for not dismissing the case. "Lord," I prayed, "give me the wisdom to answer correctly because I 'have no idea where I am going' and need you to guide me on the right road for the sake of my clients. Please help me give the answer that will save my client's case."

Now, there were only two possible responses to this Motion for Directed Verdict, and I could build a quick case for either Option A or Option B. Deciding between them was the "road" I had to choose. Ten minutes had passed, and the Judge's sheriff poked his head out of the courtroom and yelled at me, "Mr. Denny, the judge wants you back in the courtroom immediately."

I cannot tell you exactly how I settled on one of the two options for my response, but I knew that God had helped me get to the right option. I approached the Judge's bench with energy, a spring in my step, and confidence in my voice. "Judge, here is my answer to the Motion for Directed Verdict." It was a short answer—no frills, no excess verbiage, just a direct response in about three sentences. The judge smiled at me and said, "Very good, Counselor, the case goes to the jury tomorrow morning. If you had given a different answer the case would have been over." Two days later, the jury returned a very fair and just verdict in favor of my client.

Please do not misunderstand me here. I am *not* saying that The Merton Prayer is a magical incantation that always brings the results we want/need. We cannot just say this prayer three times and *abracadabra* get the right answer every time. That would be ridiculous, and The Merton Prayer is not worthy of ridicule.

I *am* saying, however, that this prayer, and especially this phrase of the prayer, focused me and in so doing defeated my fear. I clearly made the correct choice of which road to take, and the calm that came from praying The Merton Prayer helped me focus and make the right decision, which allowed my client's case not to be lost.

Consider the following scenario, so common to many of us, which is repeated on smaller scales almost daily. Imagine being one of five vice presidents of a major corporation, sitting in a planning session with your president and the other vice presidents. The president brings up the elephant in the room—a problem that you all have been losing sleep over for six months. He asks all five of his vice presidents, "So, what is the next step to get this problem fixed?" No one responds, and the president then stares directly at you, waiting for your solution to be shared with the group.

Now imagine that the words that come out of your mouth are the words of this prayer, "Mr. President, I have no idea where we are going with this problem." Methinks you would be terminated immediately, and a new person hired to take your place. This phrase of Merton is totally counter-intuitive. No vice president in charge of anything would ever admit out loud such a weakness. Yet Merton's very next phrase after invoking "My Lord God" is to zoom straight from A to Z with this incredible admission. The phrase "I have no idea where I am going" just simply cannot come out of our mouths in a situation like that, lest we be viewed as a fool who is not worthy of serious consideration on any level.

But there it is. It is this screaming admission of human vulnerability, this honest authenticity, that makes The Merton Prayer so helpful to so many people. This sentence grabs us and keeps us focused, breathlessly asking ourselves what Merton is going to say next. Can we not all admit that at so many times in our lives, at so many twists and turns on our journeys, we honestly have had no earthly idea where we are going. At this point I can hear a southern gospel preacher shouting out, "Can I get a witness?" And honest listeners holler back, "Amen! Amen! Preach it brother!"

Turn It, Turn It, Turn It

1. Think about a time when you were dumbfounded at a crossroad and just stood there, not knowing which way to go. How did it feel? What did you do to get moving? Might it not have been good to foster in yourself this sense of lostness or indecision? Perhaps that is the moment in which your heart is open to hear God's voice.

2. How have you handled those crossroad events in your life? Did it feel like you literally had no idea where you were going?

3. Should a Christ-follower always be able to know exactly and precisely where we are going? If we claim we always

know exactly where we are going, isn't that self-delusion or self-worship?

4. Are you currently in a season of life in which you are unsure of your future? If so, what could you do to connect with God during this season? What resources (a person, a community/small group, a book, a prayer, etc.) could you seek out to foster that connection with God?

5. How does Jeremiah's confession—"I know, Lord, that our lives are not our own/We are not able to plan our own course"—help you deepen or alter your own relationship with God?

III

“I Do Not See the Road Ahead of Me”

Scriptural Bases

Do not be afraid or discouraged, for the Lord will personally go ahead of you. He will be with you; he will neither fail you nor abandon you. Deuteronomy 31:8

Lead me in the right path, O Lord.... Make your way plain for me to follow. Psalm 5:8

You have made a wide path for my feet to keep them from slipping. Psalm 18:36

Show me the right path, O Lord; point out the road for me to follow.... The Lord is good and does what is right; he shows the proper path to those who go astray.... Who are those who fear the Lord? He will show them the path they should choose. Psalm 25:4, 8, 12

Look here, you who say, "Today or tomorrow we are going to a certain town and will stay there a year. We will do business there and make a profit." How do you know what your life will be like tomorrow? Your life is like the morning fog—it's here a little while, then it's gone. What you ought to say is, "If the Lord wants us to, we will live and do this or that." James 4:13-15

I pray that the eyes of your heart may be enlightened so that you may know the hope to which he has called you, the riches of his glorious inheritance in his holy people and his incomparably great power for us who believe. Ephesians 1:18-19a (NIV)

Exegesis

The subject of this sentence of The Merton Prayer is *I,* which should immediately orient us to the truth of the words. God on the other hand, being omnipotent, omniscient, and omnipresent, does indeed "see" where the road ahead of us lies. The words *do not* leave absolutely no wiggle room for me to later claim *perhaps I just had a good idea or a smart hunch* about a particular road.

To *see* always requires open eyes and a connection to our brain so that images can be processed properly. It is different than "knowing about" or "understanding" the road ahead of me. *The road ahead of me* clearly refers to an individualized travel plan, not taking some random sidetrack that may or may not be positive for me. God has a road planned out just for me, it's there, even though my eyes cannot see it.

Personal Stories

Again, how counter-intuitive it now is for we modern, enlightened, techno-savvy people to say such a thing as "I cannot see the road ahead of me." When Merton wrote these words there were no GPS systems in existence! Now, of course, all we have to do when driving in an unknown area is punch any address into our GPS app and instantly the entire road ahead of us is laid out in incredible and helpful detail. We not only can see exactly where the road goes, we also can get up-to-the-minute notices about traffic jams ten miles down the road, with accompanying alternative routes—tolls or no.

It was after 10:00 pm on a weeknight when there was a soft knock on my door. I lived in a thirteen-unit condo building and rarely, if ever, does someone knock on my door, especially late at night. Before deciding to open the door, I thought I heard sniffling. One of my neighbors, a single woman in her mid-thirties, stood there with a Kleenex at her nose. “Steven, I heard that before you were a lawyer you were a minister, is that true?”

“Yes, it is true.”

“Would you please say a prayer for me?” For the next hour she poured out her heart to me, sobbing and finally getting to the big question. She was pregnant and had made an appointment for an abortion the next morning. “What should I do?” led to “How can I do this?” which led to “I have no idea how I can be a single mom,” which finally led to “Why did God allow me to be in this position?”

At the end of our talk, I prayed for her, she thanked me, and then she told me she was *not* going to have the abortion. Now, some fourteen years later, she is still a single mom and has a fantastic son. Every time I see pictures of her with him on social media, my heart returns to the agony of her not knowing where she was going and deciding what she was going to do about her pregnancy.

I love the Casting Crowns song, “Already There,” because it captures this concept so fully: “From where I am standing, Lord, it’s so hard for me to see where this is going and where you’re leading me. I wish I knew how all my fears and all my questions are gonna play out in a world I can’t control.” Does this not mirror Merton’s “I have no idea where I am going”? And then the song’s resolution: “When I’m lost in the mystery, to you my future is a memory, cause you’re already there, standing at the end of my life, waiting on the other side."[7] (Admittedly, it may be hard to reconcile this idea of God "already there" standing at the end of my life with the image of God walking beside me every day of my life; I defer for this seeming paradox to the omnipresence of My Lord God, who is not bound by time or space.)

Many parts of my life often didn't make sense to me and often look like a jumbled mess; but I truly believe with my whole heart that God *is* the Master Painter who is creating in me a real masterpiece. I love the YouTube video of "Already There," which includes a landscape cut up into puzzle pieces that then flips and forms into a beautiful picture. The parts of our lives seem so disconnected sometimes and only in retrospect, from God's vantage point, do they fall together.

How many of us have reached a turn in our roads of life that we could never in a million years have envisioned in advance? Trusting the Lord always requires that we give up the programming of the GPS and seek God's will in every single step of the way. Even as our modern apps constantly re-route us, often many times, imagine hearing God give the directions; and also imagine knowing we are pleasing God by taking the individual path each of us is called to take.

When I was a Bible College student falling in love with Greek and Hebrew and preaching at a small church on the weekends, I could never have seen the detours God has taken me down, leading

---

7. Mark Hall, Matthew West, and Bernie Herms, "Already There" (song), *Come to the Well* (album) (Beach Street, 2011), https://castingcrowns.com/music/already-there/.

first to ordination and finally to a career in law. It was there, always "ahead of me," but unknown and unseen by me. Think about this: It was always a mystery to me, but it was always a memory to God—who was already standing at my law school graduation ceremony, watching me come down the aisle!

My mother, who was at my law school graduation, said to me after the ceremony, "Steven Alan, we always thought you would be a lawyer, the way you won all those arguments with us when you were a kid!" Her use of my middle name totally confirmed the truth of her statement. Only with 20/20 hindsight can my eyes now see how God led me on the road that resulted in my becoming a lawyer and practicing law for thirty-six years (so far).

Turn It, Turn It, Turn It

1. We in the upper Midwest are quite familiar with driving in blinding snowstorms. I recall driving from Chicago to Holland, Michigan, to see my son Jon's "away" high school basketball game, and the normally two-hour trip took over six hours because I could not even see fifteen feet of the road for long periods. How do *you* cope when there is a "life snowstorm" in front of you so that you cannot even see the road? How do *you* handle these situations? What, if any, help did you seek or get, so that you keep on that "road?" Do you ever pray to God for help in those situations? If not, why not?

2. Embrace for a moment the perspective of Moses described in Deuteronomy: *Do not be afraid or discouraged, for the Lord*

will personally go ahead of you. He will be with you; he will neither fail you nor abandon you. How might that embrace, encourage, or convict you right now in your life journey? What deep change might it provoke?

3. Acknowledge the difference between your limited vision in any given situation and God's ability to always clearly see. Does it bring a particular challenge to you? What is that challenge, and what might you do about it if you trusted God?

4. Set aside some time to evaluate and reflect upon your life, career, history of relationships, goals, successes, failures, etc. Consider if now, looking back, you realize that where you ended up is different from where you thought the road was leading. Use these discoveries as opportunities to repent, to be reassured, to forgive, and/or to give thanks to your Lord God.

5. Do the words "I do not see the road ahead of me" bring you comfort or anxiety? Might they allow you to engage with God on a deeper level than you ever have before? Share with a close friend or spiritual companion your comforts and/or anxieties.

IV

"I Cannot Know for Certain Where It Will End"

Scriptural Bases

Seek his will in all you do, and he will show you which path to take. Proverbs 3:6

"Then I bowed low and worshiped the Lord. I praised the Lord, the God of my master, Abraham, because he had led me straight to my master's niece to be his son's wife." Genesis 24:48

When I am overwhelmed, you alone know the way I should turn. Psalm 142:3

Guide my steps by your word, so I will not be overcome by evil. Psalm 119:133

The Lord directs our steps, so why try to understand everything along the way? Proverbs 20:24

Indeed, how can people avoid what they don't know is going to happen? Ecclesiastes 8:7

Exegesis

The first-person singular pronoun in this phrase of the Merton Prayer—I—always jolts me, comforts me, and reorients me to where I am in life at that moment. There clearly is Someone who *does* know for certain "where it will end," and that Someone is clearly *not* me! I may have leanings, hints, nudges—all in the direction of "certain"–but the bottom line is clear: I do not know for certain where the road I am on will end.

The word *cannot* means "I am not able," "I am not capable," and also "if I got on that road it wasn't due to any of my efforts."

The verb *to know* connotes certainty. I know that it is raining outside when I see and feel water falling from the sky. I have no doubt about that since it is confirmed by my sense of sight. *To know* is quite purposefully distinct from Merton's other verbs *to hope, to think,* and *to believe.* Keep these words and their clear differences in mind as we move through this part of the prayer.

Knowing is not guessing; it always means something is a fact. I know the road will end somewhere, both on the many and varied short roads we take while we are living and, in the long run, at the end of our lives. Is Merton referring to both short and long runs in his phrase "I do not know for certain where it will end"? He knows every road ends; he is praying that he does *not* know *where* any of them ends. "It" is the road we are on, and there is not just one "road," but many. Every single life stage or event is a road: childhood, education, career choice, marriage choice, parenthood, dealing with illness. In each of these we are on a road with twists and turns and an ending place that we cannot know about "for certain" before, and while, we are on that road. And that includes the whole shebang!

Personal Stories

In 1993, I was an associate at a small plaintiff's firm where we specialized in medical malpractice lawsuits, an area that drew much on my six years' experience working as a patient-rights ombudsman inside the Risk Management Department of a major Chicago hospital. I was second chair at a trial, which means that I was helping my boss try the case and had responsibility for questioning a few of the witnesses. The trial had already lasted for two weeks and looked to have another week or so to go.

Three months earlier I had advised my boss that my third child was due to be born right smack in the middle of the scheduled trial, and I had asked him to please seek a new trial date from the judge. He assured me that if my baby was born during the trial I could leave and he would handle the trial by himself. You know where this is going! One hour before I was to start the questioning of one of the witnesses, the Sheriff brought me a note: "your baby is coming soon, so you need to go to the hospital right now!" I showed the note to my boss, gave him the questions for the next witness, picked up my briefcase, and left the courtroom.

That night, around 7:30 pm, I received a call on the hospital phone where I was holding my beautiful new daughter Elena Marciel Denny.[8] "Congratulations on your daughter! I will see you in court tomorrow morning at 8:30." I responded, "Uhhh, no, that is not going to happen. We talked about this three months ago; I am taking a week off." Two things then quickly followed: My boss was not happy (to put it much too mildly); and I determined that my

8. Elena has stunningly gorgeous red hair just like her paternal great grandmother Rose O'Hare. I will never forget when a stranger at the supermarket saw Elena as a toddler and commented, "Oh my, she has the map of Ireland written all over her face!" My newborn had no idea the role she played in my career path, but my daughter does today.

future was not with his firm. I had no idea where or how I would exist as a "sole practitioner," but three months later I had founded "The Law Office of Steven A. Denny, P.C." God has sustained me on that road ever since.

"Not knowing for certain where a road will end" hit me square in the face in another season of my life. I certainly could not see how in 2016, when my body spent eight weeks trying to pass two kidney stones, that the Lord would use that particular road as a miracle to save my life. If I had passed those stones quickly, the aggressive prostate cancer my body already had would have taken my life within one year, according to my urologist. I had zero of the symptoms that usually accompany early diagnosis of prostate cancer. My friend and fellow-lawyer, Kevin Murphy, kidded me in week five of the stones not passing, "Hey Denny, what's the matter with you? I passed my kidney stone in less than three days!" Unbeknownst to Kevin...or to me, not passing my kidney stones saved my life. The unpassed kidney stones led to a diagnosis of aggressive prostate cancer, and one darkly humorous exchange with my doctor.

He: "You need a biopsy because your prostate feels funny."

Me: "Funny is *not* a medical term!"

So on October 31, 2016, at 6:00 am, when my wife, Miran, drove me to the hospital with "ten out of ten" kidney stone pain, I literally had no idea where that particular road was going, much less where it would end. But God did: That road led to my greatly extended life, which among many other blessings has allowed me to write this book for you. The eight weeks of pain led to a biopsy, which led to surgery, which led to radiation therapy, which led to hormone therapy, all of which have led to my being cancer free now for over five years.

I still do not "know for certain" where and when my miraculously-extended life on earth will end, but this I know with every fiber in my being: Those kidney stones were a gift from God. I am still here partly because God wants me to finish this book about The Merton Prayer that has fueled my engine for getting out of bed each morning for several years.

Turn It, Turn It, Turn It

1. Are you experiencing uncertainty about your future now? How is it affecting you? Where might God be in the midst of it? Can you give a cogent and convincing answer for what gives you a purpose for living and a meaning to your existence? If not, pray again.

2. Have you (or someone you know) ever gone down a road, maybe far down a particular road, and had to honestly admit having no idea where that road would end? Steven Covey's famous book *The Seven Habits of Highly Effective People* lists one of his essential principles for successful living as "start with the end in mind."[9] What does it mean to you when the Holy Spirit's nudging has led down a path where the likely or even the hoped-for "end in mind" was?

---

9. Steven Covey, *The Seven Habits of Highly Effective People* (Simon and Schuster, Anniversary Edition, 2013.)

3. Meditate on "The Lord directs our steps, so why try to understand everything along the way?" (Proverbs 20:24.) Allow this sentence to startle you, maybe enough to turn over more control to God.

4. Are you perhaps overwhelmed about your ultimate destiny, about death and its aftermath? What is provoking this anxiety/uncertainty? Perhaps The Merton Prayer is your opportunity to explore what God has in mind for you. Consider engaging deeply on this with a spiritual director, a spiritual companion, or a pastor, priest, minister, rabbi, imam, or guru.

5. Do you have long-term, this-worldly goals which are causing you great anxiety? If so, then consider being candid and authentic about them with God, which surely is one of the things Merton is doing with his prayer.

V

“Nor Do I Really Know Myself”

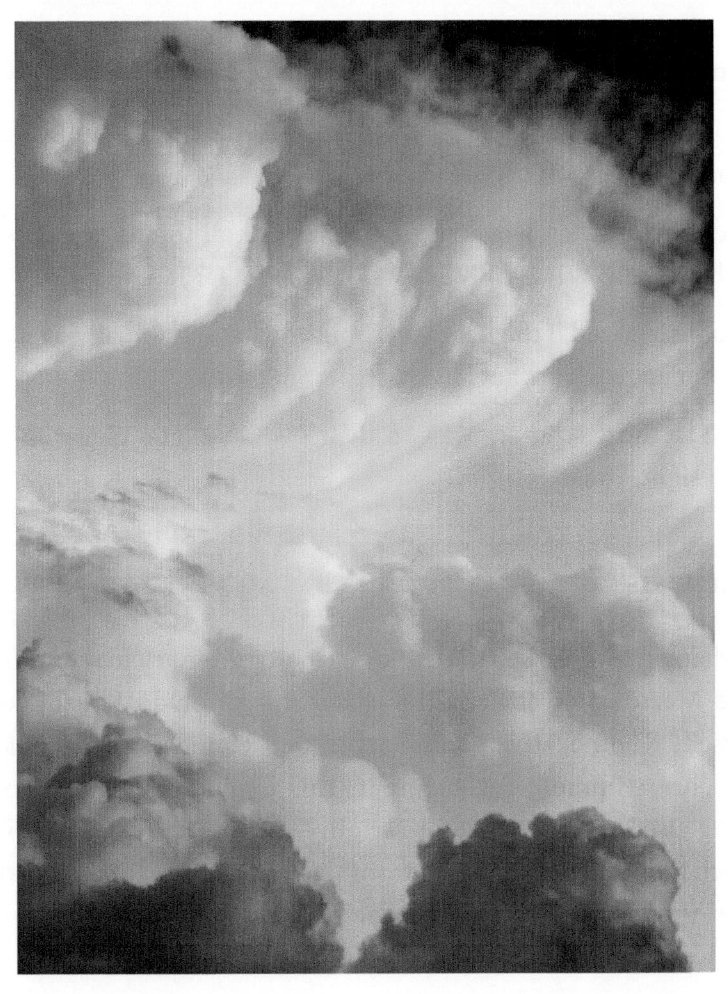

Scriptural Bases

Jesus didn't trust them, because he knew all about people. No one needed to tell him about human nature, for he knew what was in each person's heart. John 2:24-25

I don't really understand myself, for I want to do what is right, but I don't do it. Instead, I do what I hate. Romans 7:15

People may be right in their own eyes, but the Lord examines their heart. Proverbs 21:2

The human heart is the most deceitful of all things, and desperately wicked. Who really knows how bad it is? Jeremiah 17:9

Jesus said, "And if the light you think you have is actually darkness, how deep that darkness is!" Matthew 6:23b

Woe to those who are wise in their own eyes and clever in their own sight. Isaiah 5:21 (NIV)

Exegesis

Perhaps the most startling and, in my opinion, richest phrase of The Merton Prayer are these six words: "nor do I really know myself." The negative conjunctive "nor" connects this phrase to the phrase immediately before it. This signifies "and here's something else I do not know for certain—myself! The word "know" is a rich biblical word, ranging from sexual intercourse, "Adam knew Eve," (*yada'*), to "head knowledge of facts" (*oida*), and to "personally experienced known facts" (*ginosko*).

Once again, we see Merton's pure honesty in the words "nor do I really know myself." It draws me to the dichotomy of "true self" *vis-à-vis* "false self," a field of study rich with goals of helping people find and know themselves. Of course, Merton's word, *really,* is packed with meaning here: We are trained from childhood to put on a happy face when adversity strikes, but Merton will have none of that in his prayer.

We may indeed think we know who we are: I am a teacher, a truck driver, a plumber, a parent, a child, a...whatever. But Merton charges us with finding out who we "really" are, since he knows our usual *modus operandi* is so superficial it doesn't come close to the truth. Our normal internal dialogue often goes no deeper than "here's what I do for a living, or here's how I spend most of my time, so that must be who I am, right?" Hence, the subtitle of this book: "An Exercise in Authenticity," which calls for each of us to deeply analyze our identity, purpose in life, talents, and weaknesses.

Personal Stories

In addition to being a trial lawyer, I also am a certified family law mediator and founded a mediation center, "*CivilAgreement*® Mediation Services, Inc." It exists primarily so that my pastoral skills might help a couple avoid the protracted and expensive adversarial divorce process. "Mr. Denny, can you help us get a divorce; my wife has left me and says she is trying to 'find' herself?" This refrain from one husband was repeated dozens of times by other clients, both men and women, all of whom had seen their worlds collapse around them when their partners had left in search of a deeper meaning to their lives. (Or maybe just better sex.)

"Who am I?" and "why did ever I get married to this person?" and "how could I have been so stupid not to see the red flags which are so obvious now?"—these are the questions I have heard constantly in my divorce mediation practice. Aching, hurting, feeling like a failure, often led divorcing spouses to the question, "Who am *I* really?" which led many of them to the answer from The Merton Prayer: "I don't really know."

Over and over again my intake staff reported to me that such couples searching to find themselves had been married an average of nineteen years. They would sadly advise me of this fact with a shake of their heads in disbelief, "Another long-term marriage down the drain, Steven!" Correlation of the "empty-nest syndrome" with young adults moving away from home to college or their own marriage was often painfully obvious. That change in who couples thought they were resulted in a cauldron for their marriages to collapse as spouses realized that they had avoided real communication with each other for years while focusing totally on the task of raising their children.

Almost always, the spouse who sought my help viewed their now estranged wife/husband as the source of the problem. While my client might admit contributing to the demise of the marriage, his or her contribution is always presented as minor in comparison to what the awful things the other spouse has done. Rarely does this assistance-seeking spouse accept (or fully understand) the depth of his or her own culpability. "Knowing oneself," as distinct from "deceiving oneself," is never an easy job.

Implicit in this phrase of The Merton Prayer is the clear challenge that each of us ought to be able to say that I "really do know myself." I mean, how hard could it be to "really know myself," given the amazing amounts of knowledge floating around in our memory banks! Especially, also, since any bookstore has seemingly endless shelves of "self-help" books that claim to instruct us to *do* exactly what Merton says we *don't* do: namely, "really know ourselves."

I believe Merton is admitting that before an all-knowing God our self-knowledge is a ruse, created to protect our fragile ego. Or maybe we are just afraid that we might not even like the person we actually are. Only when we go deeper into learning about our true self do we stand a chance of really getting to know ourselves—and perhaps coming to peace with that person. The Jungian area of psychology abounds with documentation of the vast gulf existing between our "true self" and our "false self." Many scholars have addressed this search with great success,[10] helping the sincere seeker dodge the folly of self-deception in a quest for self-knowledge.

Among the United States Secret Service's responsibilities is protection of the U.S. currency by identifying counterfeit coins and bills. During the training to become adept at this skill, students

---

10. For example, see: Thomas Merton, *Seeds of Contemplation* (New Directions, 1949, 1987); Ruth Haley Barton, *Longing for More* (InterVarsity Press, 2007); Richard Rohr, *Falling Upward: A Spirituality for the Two Halves of Life* (Jossey-Bass, 2011) and *Immortal Diamond: The Search for Our True Self* (Jossey-Bass, 2013); and Michelle DeRusha, *True You: Letting Go of Your False Self to Uncover the Person God Created* (Baker Books, 2019).

spend the bulk of their hands-on time with real U.S. currency, and comparatively far less time with fake currency. When asked about this, an instructor said, "Only when you thoroughly know the real thing can you quickly spot the fakes!"

A good friend shared with me how his church was devastated and almost split over the discovery that their beloved and respected pastor had committed adultery with several women of the congregation. At first the church board refused to believe the rumors and reluctantly set about its "fact finding" role that included interviews of people involved. Some of the parishioners refused to accept the board's findings and recommendations, still holding to the "impossibility" of such behavior by their trusted clergyman. My friend, who was a board member during this crisis, spent much time in self-reflection with the following question: "If this warrior of the faith, my pastor who has taught, inspired, and nurtured me for years, could fall to the temptation of infidelity, might I also be vulnerable?"

This honest searching inward for answers quickly can bring us to "nor do I really know myself." The well-known adage "There but for the grace of God go I"[11] always requires the humility of authenticity as we strive for true self-knowledge. While my friend had never succumbed to infidelity, his honest look inward resulted in the humble awareness that "if my pastor could so fall, then I could

---

11. John Bradford, an English reformer who was imprisoned in the Tower of London for "stirring up a mob" and burned at the stake in 1555, is said to have coined this phrase as he watched prisoners led to their executions prior to his arrest. See: https://en.wikipedia.org/wiki/John_Bradford.

too." Merton's words here imply "how can I trust myself and my motives for my behavior if I really do not know who I am at my deepest, most personal, most vulnerable level?"

As the One who created me, My Lord God knows me from before I was even formed in the womb.[12] God knows the real me and can quickly spot the fake me, even when I have put on a masterful show of self-deceit for others. God's view of who I am, complete with the idea that I am formed in the *imago Dei* (image of God), is in a profound way the only "real" view there is.

Turn It, Turn It, Turn It

1. When was the last time you made more than a cursory inquiry into who you are and what is really happening in your life? What event or encounter thrust you into that self-examination? Have you ever felt "there but for the grace of God go I" and, if so, what insights did that bring you?

2. Go back to Jeremiah's passage at the beginning of this chapter ("The human heart is the most deceitful of all things, and desperately wicked. Who really knows how bad it is?") and chew on your own "heart condition" with brutal honesty. Not easy to do, is it? Where are you lying to God? Where are you lying to yourself?

---

12. "I knew you before I formed you in your mother's womb. Before you were born, I set you apart and appointed you as my prophet to the nations" (Jeremiah 1:5).

3. What would have to change in your life for your private and public "faces" to be fully integrated? The thought, *If they really knew xyz about me, they would never be my friend,* causes us to live an unhealthy dichotomy. Spend some time this week trying to better match your private life with your public persona. What is the first thing you might do?

4. What is blocking you from being candid, honest, and completely transparent with God (and with yourself) about who you really are? Are you ready to stop striving on your own and start waiting for God to speak to your heart?

5. Can you relate to Paul's personal dilemma above ("I don't really understand myself, for I want to do what is right, but I don't' do it. Instead, I do what I hate")? If so, know that you are not alone; many Christ-followers feel the same way as Paul did. Are you willing to be as brutally honest with yourself and God as Paul was?

VI

"And the Fact That I Think That I Am Following Your Will Does Not Mean That I Am Actually Doing So"

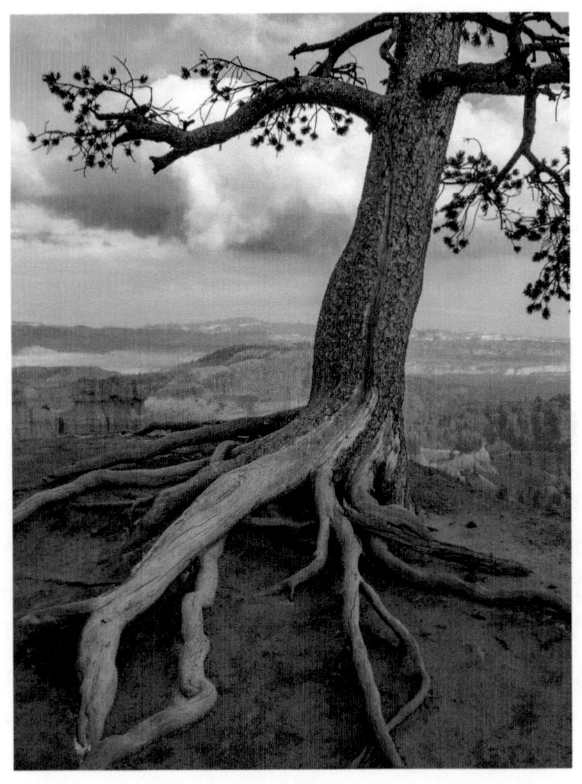

Scriptural Bases

There is a path before each person that seems right, but it ends in death. Proverbs 14:12

We can make our own plans, but the Lord gives the right answer. People may be pure in their own eyes, but the Lord examines their motives. Proverbs 16:1

We may throw the dice, but the Lord determines how they fall. Proverbs 16:33

Let's build a great city for ourselves . . . this will make us famous. . . . The Lord scattered them all over the world and they stopped building the city. Genesis 11:4-8

If we claim we have no sin, we are only fooling ourselves and not living in the truth. I John 1:8

Fools think their own way is right, but the wise listen to others. Proverbs 12:15

Exegesis

In this part of his prayer, we see Merton's honesty both refreshing and slapping us in the face with a reality check few of us ever experience. The two words *the fact* always point to our human nature and how easy it is to convince ourselves that what we are doing is following God's will. It is a "fact" that I "think I am following your will" and yet this stated "fact" does not always comport with reality.

Thinking about following God's will and "actually doing" God's will are two vastly different things. Merton wants us to hold on to this idea strongly every time we pray this phrase. The word *actually* also points out how often we can pretend to convince ourselves that what we are doing is God's will or we can simply flat out make a mistake in our analysis (as per the four Proverbs passages cited above).

Personal Stories

How easy is it for us humans to tell friends or family that "this plan I announce for my life is the Lord's will, since I prayed about it and God has answered clearly." Really? How can we know *for sure* that our plan is God's plan?

As an elder on a church board, I experienced the following awkward encounter in a very important board meeting. The board was discussing whether to retain or fire one of the pastoral staff members. The staff person in question was actually present at this meeting, sitting at the table with all of the board members; awkward, right? I suggested that the person be asked to temporarily leave the meeting so that the board members could have an honest dialogue about this serious issue.

One of my fellow board members disagreed with me and strongly advanced her position that the staff person remain in the board meeting for the discussion. She then played the "prayer trump card" and suggested that we pray about it (after all, who could object to prayer, right?). So, the board prayed.

Several board members prayed out loud, and then we got to the following prayer by the woman asking for prayer: "Lord. thank you for telling me right now that you wish for our staff member to stay in the room while we discuss this issue." I was horrified at feeling manipulated both by this "pray-er" and her "prayer." When it was my turn to pray, I said, "Thank you Lord for telling me just now that you have cancelled your previous statement to my colleague and have made it clear that the staff person should *not* stay in the room." (Some muffled sounds, bordering on giggles, emitted from a couple of board members when I "prayed" my "prayer.")

The board then concluded that the Lord had more honestly spoken through my "prayer" and asked the staff member to leave the room. Not surprisingly, I heard from my fellow board member later as she expressed her displeasure with my prayer because it had "voided" her prayer! I did not explore with her whether she honestly believed in good faith that the Lord had spoken to her, or whether she had simply engaged in wrongful conduct by attempting to manipulate the entire board. While I had indeed asked the Lord for guidance on this issue, I confess that "a word from the Lord" was not heard by me as much as my Spirit-led conviction that the staff member just had to leave the room for any honest dialogue to ensue.

Sometimes, indeed many times, old fashioned common sense aligns with the Lord's leading us. As I believe this board member illustrated, sometimes our misperception of God's will is just sinful self-deception that we manipulatively (either knowingly or unknowingly) use as a foil to exert our own will under the guise of being submissive and obedient.

This is Thomas Merton's concern. He knows we can convince ourselves so easily that *our* desires have been confirmed by the Lord, and that *our* preference is indeed *God's* will. This phrase of his prayer always smacks that nonsense out of our heads. I can "think I am following God's will" all day long but that "fact" does not mean "I am actually doing so." Humility and total surrender to the Lord is what I hear Merton asking of us with this phrase.

Sinful *hubris* is not the only spring from which a misguided sense of God's direction flows, however. A friend of mine shared how an accountant in his church felt "the call of God" to leave the accounting world, enroll in seminary, and become a pastor. The accountant was totally convinced that he was following God's will for his life, but it was a disaster. After graduating from seminary, he was hired as a pastor; but he was a very poor public speaker and quite awkward in social interactions. He left the ministry after ten years and returned to his prior vocation. This begs the question: Did the man really hear the Lord's call, or did he tragically hear only his own voice? Merton's words ring true for this accountant-turned-pastor: "And the fact that I think that I am following your will does not mean that I am actually doing so."

There is a famous prayer of the Catholic Church from Father Dolindo Ruotolo (an associate of Padre Pio) that my wife, Miran, and I often use in our times of prayer together: "Lord Jesus, I surrender myself to you; take care of everything."[13] There is also a Yiddish proverb: *Mann Tracht, Und Gott Lacht* (hear the rhyme?)

---

13. Attributed to Father Dolindo Ruotolo (1882-1970), a Neapolitan (Italian) Roman Catholic Priest.

that translates "Man plans, and God laughs." Thomas à Kempis, in his masterpiece, *The Imitation of Christ,* penned in Latin a similar adage: *Homo proponit, sed Deus disponit* ("Man proposes, but God disposes").[14] Lutheran Pastor, Dietrich Bonhoeffer, who died in a Nazi prison after having spoken out boldly against Hitler, wrote: "We must be ready to allow ourselves to be interrupted by God. God will be constantly crossing our paths and canceling our plans."[15]

Whether God cancels our plans or simply allows them to be altered by human interventions may not ever be crystal clear to us as we trip and fall into serious or even devastating situations. Many of us Christians have started down a road with full confidence we are doing what God has called us to do, only to seriously doubt later that it was anything close to a divine route we had taken. This phrase of The Merton Prayer applies to these situations.

So, the sincere question before us is this: If a road we thought was God-ordained turns out to be a disaster, did we misinterpret signs from God or did we rush ahead full steam with our plans without thoroughly vetting it with the Lord?" Ruth Everhart felt led by God after high school to attend a Christian college where she thought she would be safe. Instead of the wonderful undergraduate experience she expected and deserved, at age twenty she was raped at gunpoint. Amazingly, she survived that obscenely

---

14. Thomas à Kempis, *The Imitation of Christ* (first published about 1427), William Benham, translator (Vintage 1998).

15. Dietrich Bonhoeffer, *Life Together* (Harper Collins 1949, 1954) p. 80, https://static1. squarespace.com/static/518c65fee4b0887d9a39138d/t/5827e7aab3db2b0f3d311bf5/1479010229503/Life+Together_Eng.pdf.

horrifying event with confidence that God was leading her into Christian ministry and has written passionately about her ordeal.[16]

The church of her youth did not ordain women to ministry,[17] so she went to a seminary where women could be ordained. She obtained a Master of Divinity degree, was ordained in the Presbyterian Church, and was called by a local church to be an associate pastor in charge of "children, youth, and families." Everhart recalls that her husband and she "were ecstatic and deeply grateful to God."[18] They had every reason to believe that God had called her on *that* "road" to *that* particular congregation, where she would be their first ever female pastor. But then one day the senior pastor came into her office and assaulted her, which led to his being fired and her bringing ecclesiastical charges against him in the ecclesial court system. Her writings on these real-life events, of course, have given grace, guidance, and inspiration to many people, myself included; and clearly God has blessed the church at large with her vulnerable testimonies. But few of us would suggest that God preordained the awful roads that Ruth Everhart has traversed.

Here is a question occasioned by this phrase of The Merton Prayer: Are there times when neither I nor God see the implications of all the roads ahead of me? I leave the theology of divine omniscience to the professional theologians, while inviting you to consider the case of the prophet Jeremiah.

---

16. Ruth Everhart, *Ruined* (Tyndale House Publishers, 2016).

17. The Christian Reformed Church.

18. Ruth Everhart, *The #MeToo Reckoning* (Intervarsity Press, 2020) p. 22.

As a lawyer, I stipulate that Jeremiah was a failure in his own lifetime. Did God know all along that Jeremiah would be a failure as a prophet? How would I know? But certainly, Jeremiah must have seen his entire life's work as a failure. Yet we cannot truly measure the meaning of a person's life (or career) only by the disappointments and failures. God used Jeremiah in unexpected ways to save the Hebrew people from despair. Jeremiah showed them (and us today) that God's throne is not confined to the temple and, therefore, the demise of the temple by invading armies did not mean the end of God's reign over all the Earth. How huge is that? I believe that an outcome that God may not have preordained may still be a road that leads to outcomes that please God greatly. But then, I'm no theologian; I'm giving you "just the facts, Ma'm" as I (and perhaps channeling Sergeant Friday of the old TV show *Dragnet)* see them.

Victor Frankl's famous *Man's Search for Meaning*[19] addressed the questions he and other survivors of the Nazi concentration camps faced during World War II. Prisoners who asked, "Why has God allowed this to happen to me?" often did not survive their horrendous ordeal; whereas survivors seemed to be asking, "How can I take these circumstances and find ways to make a difference?" The former question led to despair, immobilization, and death, whereas the latter question led to a life-sustaining purpose. Clearly God did not "preordain" Hitler to create concentration camps, yet even in the worst of circumstances God's presence can be transformative.

---

19. Victor E. Frankl, *Man's Search for Meaning* (Beacon Press, 2006).

This is what I think Merton is trying to get at in this part of his prayer: We shouldn't be so sure we know what God has in mind for us, but we can be confident that God knows. As St. Justin Martyr put it about two millennia ago, "With God, nothing is impossible," or as a more contemporary saying might render, "It is impossible to overestimate God, because then—by definition—whatever you are overestimating is not God."

Turn It, Turn It, Turn It

1. How did you deal with a situation where you convinced yourself that you were following God's will, only to be firmly convinced later that it was not God's will but your own will? Have you decided going forward in life how you can be more confident in discerning God's will for your life?

2. Read and reflect on Genesis 11:1-9 (The Tower of Babel). Are there religious endeavors or behaviors that you currently practice that are only rooted in tradition or habit, which lack intentionality and depth on your part? What would it mean for you to become sincere, intentional, or purposeful in that spiritual practice?

3. What are some new spiritual practices which might foster in you a more authentic Christian walk with the Lord? What is stopping you from considering and implementing these practices?

4. Do you have some trusted and mature Christian friends to whom you can turn for "evaluation" and possible "confirmation" of whether or not your plan is "of God?" Make a list of who they are and then act on it.

5. Meditate on the above quote from Dietrich Bonhoeffer ("We must be ready to allow ourselves to be interrupted by God. God will be constantly crossing our paths and canceling our plans.") Do you "allow" such "interruptions" and "cancelations" to be from God or do you push them aside as your own failures and mistakes? How would your journey be altered if you did indeed give God the glory for the detours and blocked roads as well as the smooth highways?

VII

"But I Believe That the Desire to Please You Does in Fact Please You"

Scriptural Bases

May the Lord give us the desire to do his will in everything. I Kings 8:58

For you look deep within the mind and heart, O righteous God. Psalm 7:9b

May he grant your heart's desires and make all your plans succeed. Psalm 20:4

Give your burdens to the Lord, and he will take care of you. He will not permit the godly to slip and fall." Psalm 55:22

Whom have I in heaven but you? I desire you more than anything on earth. Psalm 73:25

And it is impossible to please God without faith. Anyone who wants to come to him must believe that God exists and that he rewards those who sincerely seek him. Hebrews 11:6

Exegesis

The little adversative word *but* is the turning point in The Merton Prayer, the fulcrum upon which rests the answer, the antidote, to the awful pain and despair of the prayer's preceding phrases. Think of it this way: We have just articulated such hopelessness and helplessness with honest words such as "I don't know where I am going, I cannot see the road ahead of me, I don't know where this road ends, I don't even know myself." After those words of truthful despair comes riding to the rescue this little "but."

An adversative in grammatical terms always signals a change, often canceling out everything that just preceded it. That's why it is called an "adversative;" it always signals the *adverse,* a word meaning "acting against or in a contrary direction." For example, "I like that new outfit you are wearing, but the colors don't do your complexion justice;" "I love you sweetheart, but here are the forty-eight things which I would like to see you change." See what I mean? After the "but," the words before are modified, canceled, revised, or clarified in some way. That's why a true apology can never contain the word *but*: "I'm so sorry the church did not protect your child from the pedophile, but...." That little word carries huge significance, as it does here in The Merton Prayer.

When I presented a seminar on The Merton Prayer to a group of Christian lawyers, I dared to give vent to my silly side by adopting at this point the lyrics of a then-popular (slightly off-color) song my kids had (unfortunately) introduced me to: "I like big *buts* and I cannot lie!"[20] The folks under forty in the room howled with laughter, while those over sixty looked at me with scowls on their faces until I quickly advised them that my "buts" only had one "t." Then they kinda smiled, *but* they never came close to howling!

The little word *but* turns everything around in this prayer. Indeed, I cannot lie about how important this little bitty word is to me, and I hope to all who encounter this prayer. Up until now Merton has forced us to a place of genuine authenticity, a place we rarely encounter, rarely enjoy, and quickly exit when it falls

20. Parodying the song by Anthony L. Ray (Sir Mix-a-Lot), "Baby Got Back" (song), *Mack Danny* (album) (Def American Recordings, 1992).

over us like a cloud of despair. Following this "but" we see light, we see hope, we see a path to please God which we have likely never considered previously. This "but," takes us in a whole different direction, down a different road, with a completely different orientation. After this "but," nothing can ever be the same as it was before.

The next two words in the prayer, "I believe," are interesting since they contrast with the words "does in fact" that come later. Here Merton shares his vulnerable "belief," and I can almost hear him thinking aloud during his times of silent prayer at Gethsemani: *I sure hope this is true what I am about to say; yes, I believe it in my heart and share it right here in this prayer so that others may believe it as well.*

Belief and *knowledge* are two different things, are they not? How would it sound to us if Merton had said "but I *know* that the desire to please you does in fact please you"? Audacious and presumptive, right? The word *believe,* on the other hand, rings true to the context, falling right after the hugely significant and adversative "but."

I love the C. S. Lewis quote that my niece Wendy Herrberg has inscribed on the wall in her Indiana kitchen for her family and guests to chew on (while also chewing on her great meals): "I believe in Christianity as I believe that the sun has risen, not only because I see it but because *by* it I see everything else."[21] This kind of belief gives great power to all the remaining assertions in this

---

21. C. S. Lewis, "They Asked For A Paper," in *Is Theology Poetry?* (London: Geoffrey Bless, 1962) pp. 164-165.

phrase of The Merton Prayer.

"Desire" is different from completed action. I "desire" to run a marathon in under three hours, but the chance of that happening (post three knee surgeries) is so remote it is not within the realm of possibility. Whether our actions actually do *please* God is not the question for Merton. We don't even know what the word means in this context, since it attributes a human emotion (pleasure) to God.

We have been assured in Genesis, however, that God knows us so intimately that we are made in the *imago Dei.* God, whom it is impossible to overestimate, knows our strengths, our weaknesses, our lip-service to change and transformation. How totally comforting it is, therefore, to also believe that God could actually be "pleased" by our desire to please God.

Now, however, comes the bombshell. Our "belief" now becomes "in fact" in The Merton Prayer! This change is so powerful it knocks my theological socks off every single time I read it or recite it. Our desires, hopes, plans, to please God with actions that are pure, honest, and non-duplicitous, do "in fact" please God. Thank you, Thomas Merton, for such an incredible hope-filled assertion! Including the two little words "in fact" adds such power to your prayer. Read the phrase without "in fact" and see how weak it sounds. "That's a fact, Jack" hits me every time I get to this phrase. No doubts are left from my "belief," according to Merton. When God sees that I have "desired" to please, it is indeed ("in fact") a done deal.

How does Merton know that God is pleased? Well, he doesn't really say, but I am reminded of the scene in the movie *A Christmas*

Story ("you'll shoot your eye out") when the father asks Ralphie if Santa had asked him if he'd been a good boy. Ralphie shrugs and says, "I dunno," but the father says, "Oh, Santa knows. Santa *always* knows." We might say "We dunno" if God is pleased with our intentions, but Merton says it is a matter of fact: "Oh, God is pleased. God is always pleased."

Personal Stories

No one is sinless, as Paul said in Romans 3:23: "For everyone has sinned; we all fall short of God's glorious standard." How can I in my sinfulness ever hope to "please" God? Think about how much ink has been spilled over this issue of our failure to live up to God's standards. Depression abounds in the human heart of anyone who tries and tries to please God and fails miserably.

In Merton's own life there were failures and flaws which clearly informed this phrase of the prayer. His biographers have written that he fathered a child out of wedlock while a student at Cambridge University before becoming a Catholic and a Trappist monk.[22] He is also supposed to have had an inappropriate relationship with a young female nurse when he was a patient at a Louisville hospital, a relationship that apparently continued after

22. Paul Elie, *The Life You Save May be Your Own* (Farrar, Straus, and Giroux, 2003) pp. 41-42; Robert Inchausti, *Thinking Through Thomas Merton: Contemplation for Contemporary Times* (SUNY Press, 2014) p. 9; and David E. Orberson, *Thomas Merton—Evil and Why We Suffer: From Purified Soul Theodicy to Zen* (Cascade Books, 2018).

his discharge.[23] Keep these "allegations" of fact about Merton's life fully in mind as you process this phrase. Significantly flawed are all human beings, in desperate need of God's forgiveness and redemption; and if our "desires to please God" do indeed please God, well, how startling and fantastic is that?

How comforting it is to my aching human spirit to pray this phrase and believe it in my deepest soul: "Oh Lord, I believe that the *desire* to please you, *does in fact* please you." Implicit in that phrase is this: my desire may not come anywhere close to matching the reality of my actions. The passage from Paul's letter to the Romans quoted above is printed on the calling card for every human being, since *not a single one of us* can walk on Earth without sin. For me, with this phrase The Merton Prayer reaches its highpoint of power and comfort. I have heard so many sermons condemning me to hell for actions I have confessed over and over and behaviors I repeated with full knowledge that I was sinning, but few words have been sent my way encouraging me with the truth expressed in these simple words of Thomas Merton.

The amazing idea that God could in fact "be pleased" by my intentions and desires was totally new to me until I read The Merton Prayer, and it is something that has given me powerful hope every day since. As a child, I sat under teachers and preachers who convinced me that the *only* way I could "please" God was by

23. Mark Shaw, *Beneath the Mask of Holiness: Thomas Merton and the Forbidden Love Affair that Set Him Free* (St. Martin's Press, 2009); Suzanne Zuercher, *The Ground of Love and Truth: Reflections on Thomas Merton's Relationship with the Woman Known as "M"* (In Extenso Press, an imprint of ACTA Publications, 2014).

successfully avoiding *all* sin. This phrase of The Merton Prayer has eviscerated such juvenile nonsense for me, and I hope it does for you as well. St. Josemaria Escriva (founder of Opus Dei) taught that a saint is not someone who does not fall but someone who always gets up trusting in God:

> You are full of weaknesses. Each day you see them more clearly. But don't let them frighten you.... Your involuntary falls—a child's falls—show your Father-God that he must take more care.... Each day as our Lord picks you up from the ground, take advantage of it, embrace him with all your strength and lay your wearied head on his open breast so that you will be carried away by the beating of his most lovable Heart.[24]

During his extensive training in preparation for the 1924 Paris Summer Olympics, Scottish athlete Eric Liddell (the subject of the Academy Award-winning film *Chariots of Fire)* was criticized by some for wasting time with competitive running and thereby delaying his move to China to become a missionary for Jesus. Responding to such critics, Liddell said, "I believe that God made me for a purpose. But he also made me fast and, when I run, I feel God's pleasure."[25] Many runners ran in Paris that summer, with the usual motivations of competing to win a medal for their home country. Eric Liddell ran with the motivation of pleasing God. I am reminded

24. Josemaria Escriva, "Life of Childhood," in *The Way* (Scepter Press, 2001) p. 884.

25. Colin Welland (writer), *Chariots of Fire* (movie) (Warner Brothers, 1981).

here of the dialogue between God and the fictional Mackenzie Phillips in *The Shack*[26] when God repeatedly tells Mack, "I am especially fond of you." That idea encourages me daily to "desire to please God."

Dr. Stephen Hufman, whose photographs accompany the words of Merton's prayer in this book, has written about how one of his patients named Lester (not his real name) suffered from drug addiction and came in asking the doctor for a prescription for opioids.[27] He had no hope of overcoming his addiction and threatened "suicide by cop" if he didn't get what he wanted. Lester looked much older than his age, ravaged by the effects of drugs, with unkempt scraggly beard, wrinkled leathery face, clothes reeking of tobacco, yellow and many missing teeth. Unknown to Dr. Hufman at this initial encounter was the life-long pain of having been molested by an uncle and forced into prostitution to pay for drugs, along with many stays in jail. Lester was clearly experiencing withdrawal symptoms and begged for "Percs, White Stuff, or—better yet—give me methadone."

When Dr. Hufman advised him that he would only prescribe methadone if Lester agreed to enter a rehab program for addicts, Lester pulled a bowie knife out of his pocket and threatened to either kill the doctor or kill himself due to his desperation and fear of being sent back to jail. His fear was real since Lester had spent much time in and out of jail.

---

26. William P. Young, *The Shack* (Windblown Media, 2007). Also, the movie by the same title.

27. Stephen L. Hufman, MD, *A Desperate Need: A Guide to Treating Addictions and Recapturing Life* (To Serve and Encourage Publications, 2019).

What ensued was a Christian doctor talking a junkie down from harming himself or others, while sharing the Gospel in a way that actually reached Lester. He not only agreed to enter the program; he also promised to see a Christian counselor whom Dr. Hufman recommended and to read daily some Bible verses Hufman gave him. (Only later did Dr. Hufman discover that Lester could not read but had to ask his counselor to read the scripture passages to him.)

Lester eventually became a "new man in Christ," and his countenance warmed all who met him. His testimony was especially powerful and encouraging to all who knew his history. Lester "desired to please God" with every ounce of his being. During his rehab treatment, he was found to have terminal lung cancer, but even that did not diminish his joy in the slightest, as he told Dr. Hufman in their last chat:

> Now that I have terminal cancer, I've found life in dying, like that thief on the cross next to Jesus. My hope in Jesus covers everything with life, even my approaching death. I'm not afraid anymore with Jesus.[28]

Turn It, Turn It, Turn It

1. How much energy do you put into "desiring" to please God with your thoughts and actions? The old adage "to fail to plan is to plan to fail" applies here, if we are to enjoy peace around

---

28. Stephen L. Hufman, MD, *A Desperate Need: A Guide To Treating Addictions and Recapturing Life* (To Serve and Encourage Publications, 2019) p. 11.

this "fulcrum" point of The Merton Prayer. This week, what can you do to proactively plan to please God?

2. In this phrase, we find Merton changing from candid and sobering self-assessment to *confidence* and *hope* in the pursuit of God. Where is your focus when it comes to planning out your desired-for outcomes in life? Reflect on your spiritual intentions and motivations.

3. Are you now in a moment in which you are in need of "always desiring to please God"? Could God be using The Merton Prayer to invite you into such a real reformation of your spiritual life? Consider and engage the resources you may need for this reformation (e.g., books, prayer, spiritual director, pastoral counselor, small accountability group).

4. Reflect deeply on the passage from Hebrews: "And it is impossible to please God without faith. Anyone who wants to come to him must believe that God exists and that he rewards those who sincerely seek him." How does this truth (that God accepts our faith and our sincere pursuit of him) encourage, challenge, or confuse you?

5. Spend some time with the quote from I Kings: "May the Lord give us the desire to do his will in everything." Have you ever truly asked God to re-orient your desires? If so, what were the consequences? If not, consider the good that could come from uttering such a prayer. Then do it daily for at least one month.

VIII

"And I Hope I Have That Desire in All That I Am Doing"

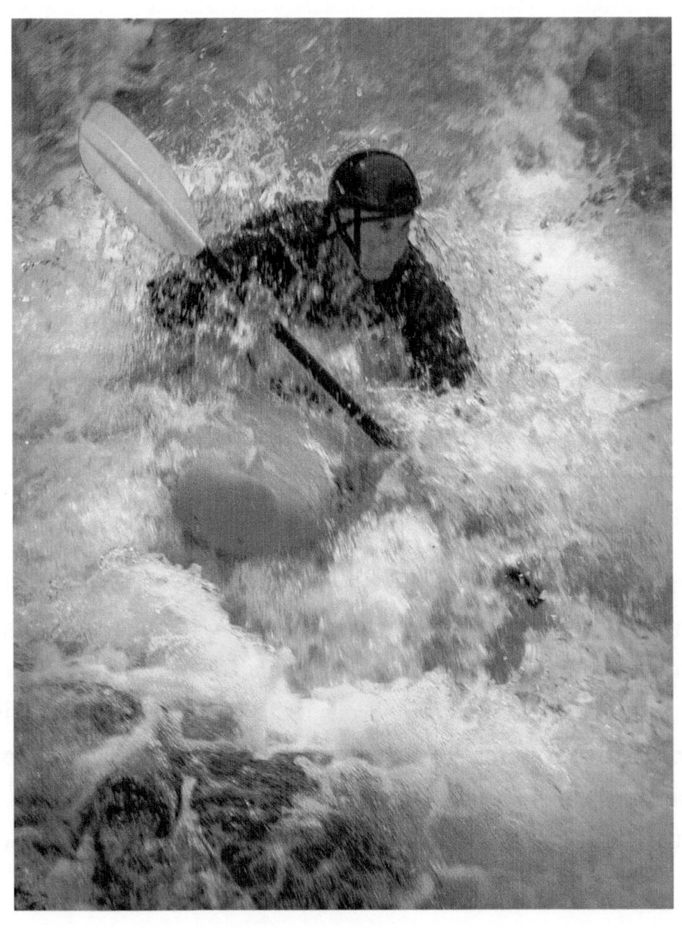

Scriptural Bases

Those who live to please the Spirit will harvest everlasting life from the Spirit. Galatians 6:8b

For God is working in you, giving you the desire and the power to do what pleases him. Philippians 2:13

"Wherever your treasure is, there the desires of your heart will also be." Matthew 6:21

Now may the God of peace...equip you with all you need for doing his will. May he produce in you, through the power of Jesus Christ, every good thing that is pleasing to him. Hebrews 13:20-21

Take delight in the Lord, and he will give you your heart's desires. Psalm 37:4

Our purpose is to please God, not people. He alone examines the motives of our hearts. I Thessalonians 2:4b

Exegesis

To start a sentence with the conjunction *and* is usually *verboten* in English grammar, but Merton does it twice in his prayer. Lest we, his readers, should fail to connect the previous phrase with what follows, the word *and* forces us to equate these two phrases into one. It is not enough for us only to "believe that the desire to please God does in fact please God." The "and" makes us zoom into the next phrase without pausing, thereby feeling in our gut the connection. Yes, believe it, *and* then "I hope I have that desire in all that I am doing."

With the word *hope* Merton has taken us into the arena of possibility, connecting this "I hope" to the "I believe" statement preceding it. The word *hope* means "to cherish a desire with anticipation, to want something to happen or to be true, to desire with expectation of obtainment or fulfillment."[29] I love the above definition's use of "to cherish," since this phrase of the prayer invites us to "cherish" the thought that we *could* have the desire to please God in every thought and action of our life.

"That desire," of course, refers to the desire to please God. The word *all* encompasses the entirety of life, leaving no room for any behavior that is not pleasing to God. Think about the phrase "I am doing." It is a present tense verb, which signifies the "here and now" of life. The past is done, over with, not able to be changed. If I have, in the past, *not* sought to please God in "all that I [was] doing," that behavior is something I can leave behind in the past and repent of in the present. If that past behavior was composed of efforts to please God, those efforts can be the basis of a virtue or habit of desiring to please God in the present and future. *Hope*, as it is used in The Merton Prayer, always points to the present and to the future. What a relief that is to all of us sinners.

---

29. "Hope," Merriam-Webster.com Dictionary (Merriam-Webster, 2020), https://www. merriam-webster.com/dictionary/hope.

Personal Stories

I could spend the rest of my life reading and rereading Merton's words in so many of his books. They often surprise me with new insights so profound that I gasp and, like an old-fashioned record player getting stuck in the same spot, perseverate on a phrase for days. Here's one, also from *Thoughts in Solitude* (where The Merton Prayer comes from): "A life is either all spiritual or not spiritual at all. No man can serve two masters. Your life is shaped by the end you live for. You are made in the image of what you desire."[30] What? Me? I am *"made in the image of what I desire?"* Seriously? I thought I was made in the image of God. Notice what Merton has done here, connecting our "desires to please God" in his prayer with "the end we live for," namely, pleasing God in everything we do.

So, this phrase of the prayer catapults me to the bottom of a high mountain peak where I ask myself regularly, "Steven, do you truly desire to please God in *everything* you are doing?" This always and quickly becomes a very sobering climb up that mountain for sure! Every thought, every action, every second of every hour—is it really possible to achieve this high goal of always pleasing God? To live in such a way is to "take captive every thought to make it obedient to Christ" as Paul encourages us to do in 2 Corinthians 10:5 (NIV).

Robert Lavelle was a Christian and a banker who lived and worked in Pittsburgh, Pennsylvania. Pittsburgh's faith community

---

30. Thomas Merton, *Thoughts in Solitude* (Farrar, Straus, Giroux Publishing, 1956, 1958, 1999) p. 49.

has a history of finding ways to live out the implications of Christ's Kingdom of God in all aspects of life. For Lavelle, that meant finding the convergence of banking, community, and Jesus' heart. As a result, in 1969 he opened the Dwelling House Savings & Loan in the Hill District neighborhood of Pittsburgh, a predominantly Black neighborhood which had been ignored by financial institutions. He saw the need for financial services and advice to those who had never had an opportunity to get a loan or open a savings account.

Lavelle's bank offered loans to those who were viewed as "high risk" and/or "not worth my time" by other bankers. In contrast to the few businesses that did venture into the area, he chose not to install garage-door-like bars on his bank building. Lavelle viewed himself and his institution as called by God to 1) be a member of the neighborhood, 2) serve his neighbors, and 3) live out his Christian faith in all of life.[31] Unfortunately, the bank closed in 2009 following the dire economic crisis of 2008, but Lavelle's legacy and witness remain vital to Pittsburg and beyond. He had the "desire to please God" in every aspect of his life.

My brother, Gerald Denny, has been a pastor for sixty-two years and is truly one of my heroes. He was an all-star high school and college athlete with a Kentucky High School basketball state championship to his credit. I recall, as a ten-year-old, asking my twenty-year-old brother–who was already, at that young age, a

31. See Robert Wauzzinski, "In God We Trust," in *Third Way* (April 1987); and Robert Wauzzinski, *The Transforming Story of Dwelling House Savings and Loan* (Edwin Melon Press, 2003).

youth minister for a church in Illinois— "Gerald, I know that you will make it into heaven, but do you think any of the rest of our family will be there with you?"

Gerald and his wife, Ruth, have spent the last forty-four years with Pioneer Bible Translators (PBT), first as board members and then as a full-time staff providing pastoral care for the missionaries of PBT, a wonderful ministry located in Dallas, Texas. Their work has taken them to many countries around the globe for "on-site" pastoral care with the missionaries who have been called to put God's word into languages where no Bibles have ever existed and often where written forms of the spoken languages have never existed.

Gerald's comments about this phrase in The Merton Prayer are powerful and worth sharing: "Hoping to have the desire to please God in all that I do leads me to self-examination. As I look at all the things I have done in the last week, can I honestly say each was done with the conscious desire to please God?" He starts each workday by asking the Holy Spirit: "What do you want us to do together today?" Whatever things the Holy Spirit brings to Gerald's mind are the things that "go on our 'to do' list for that day." He then asks the Holy Spirit for guidance on prioritizing the tasks; after finishing the first task, he goes on to the second task, and so forth. Then at the end of the day, he takes inventory of what he and the Holy Spirit have accomplished together.

I think my brother epitomizes the need to constantly examine our intentions and the motivation behind our words and actions while trying to grow in purity of heart. Gerald's practice reminds me of the spiritual discipline known as the daily Examen or Examination of Conscience, which helps us see where we either encountered or missed God during the past twenty-four hours. I have practiced the Examen for almost twenty years, journaling about where I saw or failed to see (missed) God each day. Many nights I climb out of bed after realizing I have not yet made notes of my daily Examen. I highly recommend this spiritual exercise.[32] The next phrase of the prayer will add extra ammunition to Merton's "hoped-for" request to always desire to be God-pleasing.

My brother-in-law, Dean Dickinson, is the pastor who gave what is called "the charge" at my ordination to Christian ministry. One of his usual corporate prayers includes these challenging and simple words, "Lord please help us be willing to be willing." Hoping to please God in "all that I am doing" surely requires me to be "willing to be willing."

Turn It, Turn It, Turn It

1. The Merton Prayer's honesty allows you to evaluate whether or not your plans and actions are focused on pleasing God or pleasing yourself. Make sacred space this week to sit with this self-inquiry: In the past few days, what did you do that you hoped pleased God and when did you miss chances to do so?

---

32. For good overviews and introduction to "The Examen," see: Mark E. Thibodeaux, *Reimagining the Ignatian Examen: Fresh Ways to Pray from Your Day* (Loyola Press, 2014); and Timothy M. Gallagher, *The Examen Prayer: Ignatian Wisdom for Our Lives Today* (Crossroad Publishing, 2006).

2. Read and reflect on St. Paul's advice: "Take captive every thought to make it obedient to Christ" (2 Corinthians 10:5). Identify any thoughts which have yet to be yielded to God (which Alcoholics Anonymous calls "stinking thinking").

3. For the next week try to include the Examen spiritual discipline in your nightly prayer time. How did you encounter God or miss God in the past day? Pay attention to where the Holy Spirit leads you during the next day and compare that to your "catchings" and "missings" of the previous day.

4. Dig deeply into the Philippians passage above: "For God is working in you, giving you the desire and the power to do what pleases him." Do you see any evidence that God is working in you or you are working in God? If so, what consequences can you identify? If not, what might be preventing you from desiring to please God?

5. Do Paul's words above in Hebrews bring you comfort in knowing that God will "equip you" for what you need to please God? "Now may the God of peace...equip you with all you need for doing his will." For the next week, can you pray daily for God to "produce in you" only "good things that are pleasing" to God? If so, try to do it.

IX

“I Hope That I Will Never Do Anything Apart from That Desire”

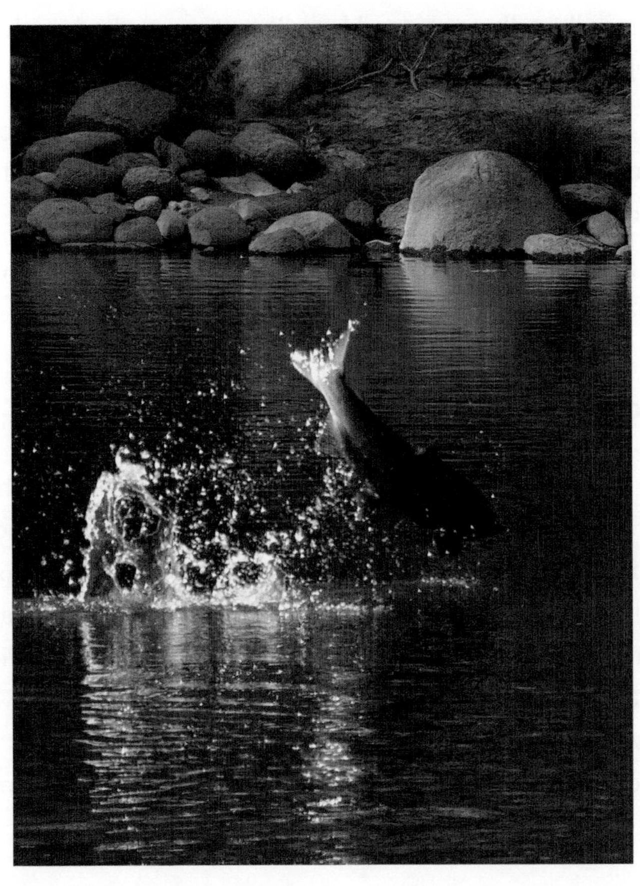

Scriptural Bases

"Seek ye first the kingdom of God and his righteousness." Matthew 6:33 (KJV)

Carefully determine what pleases the Lord. Ephesians 5:10

For God is working in you, giving you the desire and the power to do what pleases him. Philippians 2:13

Seek his will in all you do, and he will show you which path to take. Proverbs 3:6

"If any of you wants to be my follower, you must give up your own way, take up your cross daily, and follow me. If you try to hang on to your life, you will lose it." Luke 9:23-4

Never be lacking in zeal, but keep your spiritual fervor, serving the Lord. Romans 12:11

Exegesis

In this passage from The Merton Prayer, we encounter the exercise of more of our "hope" being aimed at that high mountain peak of never doing *anything* apart from the desire to please God. This phrase of the prayer essentially is the negative restatement of Merton's previous positive phrase. The positive, "having this desire to please God in all I am doing," is here contrasted with the negative "never" of this phrase.

The goal of always being pleasing to God is so intimidating that Merton restates the request, just in case we miss the essence of the entire prayer. "Never" leaves no room for *any* behavior which is not pleasing to God. "Anything" also leaves no room for wriggling. "Apart from" reorients us to the source of God-pleasing behavior. Only with conscious focus on pleasing God can we ever expect to experience this particular "hope" becoming reality.[33] We are reaching the end of the line here. We either get off at this stop or we are going to continue to the end of the line, confident that The Merton Prayer's next phrases can bring incredible peace and comfort

Personal Stories

Here we go again, as if in a courtroom:

Judge: What does it mean to please God in everything, Counselor? It is humanly impossible, right?

Attorney: Yes, Your Honor, but St. Paul says, "Christ in you [is] the hope of glory."[34] We are called to be conforming ourselves more and more to Jesus, the Son of God, and thus becoming through Christ children of God. This is the work of the Holy Spirit in our soul. It is the work of a lifetime. Christian tradition calls it "identification with Christ" and "sanctification." St. Ignatius' phrase, "For the greater glory of God," and St. Escriva's invocation,

---

33. Merton's thought here is similar to ideas found in Brother Lawrence. See *Excerpts from The Practice of The Presence of God* in *Devotional Classics*, R.J. Foster & J.B. Smith, editors, (Harper, San Francisco 1993), especially pp. 81-84.

34. Colossians 1:27.

"All the Glory to God," surely encourage us toward lives pleasing to God, knowing that the Holy Spirit and "Christ in us" is really our only hope.

Judge: OK. So ruled.

Attorney: Thank you, Your Honor.

When I contemplate the goal of living a God-pleasing life in all that I do, the temptation to just admit abject failure is such an easy option. Recently, driving on a Chicago freeway, a driver dangerously cut in front of me. My reaction was to yell, "What a jerk." (That is the cleaned-up version.) I wrongly thought my outcry was heard only by my wife, the only other person in the car. Immediately, however, the omnipresent Siri in my phone spoke up through the car speaker system loudly with curt clarity, "That's not nice, Steven."

Really? Oh, my goodness, my wife and I were both horrified. Substitute God for Siri (not orthodox theology, I grant you) and you see where this is going. If I cannot even please my phone's inanimate algorithm, how can I hope to please My Lord God—all the time, in every word, and in every action?

Pleasing God in my efforts as a trial lawyer is certainly not always easy. When an opposing lawyer stood in open court and lied to the judge that I had agreed to a certain deposition date, it was not by my own spirit that I refrained from lashing out in anger. My tempered response, without calling him a liar, "I recall our conversation differently, and from now on I will only speak with this lawyer in the presence of a third party." This led him to file a motion to "compel" me to answer his phone calls and talk to him whenever he wished. For the only time in my legal career, I cited my First Amendment rights to freedom of speech and association. The judge ruled in my favor (with a smile on his face) while the opposing attorney scowled and walked out of the courtroom.

I had a five-day trial representing a woman who fractured her hip while walking on a city sidewalk because there were construction defects in the concrete that caused her to fall. I documented that the city had been told of the defects for over two years but had never come to do the simple repairs. It was a strong case, in my humble opinion. I worked hard getting my client ready for her trial testimony and was very confident that she would do a good job. The medical witnesses and engineering expert I had hired all gave very clear and powerful testimony. Both my opening and closing statements had gone well.

My client did a good job in her testimony as I took her through the tortuous memories of her fall, her medical treatment, and her current condition of daily pain. I had shown the jurors her medical records, blown up on large exhibits. The jury got the case for deliberation at 12:30 pm and my client, my paralegal, and I walked three blocks to a nearby restaurant for lunch.

The quickest I have ever had a jury return a verdict was three hours; this jury set a new record. We had ordered our food, but it had not yet arrived at our table when I got the phone call from the judge's clerk. "Mr. Denny, the jury has returned a verdict. Please come back to the courtroom immediately." With tempered and skeptical, but somewhat justified, optimism, we all walked back to the courthouse. When the jury was brought into the courtroom, none of them looked at my client or me. That is the universal trial lawyer's worst nightmare: A jury who has voted in favor of your client *always* looks right at the plaintiff (and at you) when they have reached a favorable verdict.

The jury's verdict was "not guilty" (which meant my client had lost her case). In a state of shock, I told her that I wanted to speak with the jurors when they were released from the jury room, and that she should go home and I would call her later. Three jurors came up to me and initiated conversation, not the usual post-trial-chat *modus operandi* for jurors, who usually just want to go home. One of them said, "Mr. Denny, all twelve of us loved your case and were ready to vote in your favor; but we noticed in the medical records that your client had given two different social security numbers when she was admitted at different hospitals. One of our jurors said, 'that is welfare fraud,' which meant that we could not trust your client's testimony. Sorry."

I was flabbergasted by this information. I grabbed my two large blowup exhibits of her hospital admissions and, indeed, two very different social security numbers were recorded for her admission records. I had never noticed this, nor had I ever considered confirming social security numbers on all medical records of my client's treatment, since welfare fraud is not something that I routinely checked for with *any* of my clients. I called my client later and learned that she had been obtaining double disability benefits tied to the different social security numbers. The jurors were correct, and she had indeed been committing fraud on the system, rendering her non-credible about how she had been injured.

A major ethical rule for attorneys is this: Never allow a client to present false testimony under oath. I had not "purposely" presented false testimony, and as far as I had known my client's description of how she was injured was true; nevertheless, jurors are allowed to conclude that a witness who is caught in a lie about one thing may be lying about other things, including the facts of how she was injured. This jury had very quickly followed the instructions given them by the judge and rendered a verdict against my client.

My failure to properly prepare for trial meant that I had acted in a way that could not possibly have "pleased God." In whatever career we pursue, our daily job as a Christ-follower always means that "we work as unto the Lord" or, as my friend Mark Davies, a corporate vice-president, says in his adaptation of Colossians 3:23, "We play only to an audience of One."[35] It was my fault entirely for not having observed the problem prior to moving ahead into a trial. I felt terrible because I had wasted the resources of the Cook County Circuit Court by even bringing this case to trial.[36]

My sister, Jana Denny Dickinson, is another of my spiritual heroes. I view her Christian witness as impeccably strong and

---

35. "Whatever you do, work at it with all your heart, as working for the Lord, not for human masters" (Colossians 3:23 NIV).

36. I actually wrote a letter to the judge apologizing for bringing the case into his courtroom. One of my attorney friends told me months later that, when an attorney in that same courtroom had failed to adhere to the rules, the judge picked up my letter (which he obviously had kept close by on the bench for just such a situation), read it to the packed courtroom full of attorneys, and said something to this effect: "Here is how an ethical attorney responds when he makes a mistake." Interesting how God can take one of our failures and weave a positive message for others.

powerful for living the life of a Christian "saint" called to be in the world but not of the world. She taught Sunday School for years, has written articles in Christian periodicals, and was on the Board of Directors of Lincoln Christian University, where she and I and our brother Gerald had all attended. She taught elementary school for twenty-eight years and is married to a wonderful minister, Dean Dickinson; the two of them have worked in ministry together for over fifty years.

I grew up, with the eyes of an adoring younger brother, believing that my sister Jana was "perfect" and never did anything mischievous (as her little brother, me, was wont to do). When I asked Jana recently if this phrase of The Merton Prayer spoke to her in any way, she shared the following. "Steven, I accepted Christ as my savior at the age of eight,[37] and I have had the *desire* to serve him ever since. But *desire* doesn't always manifest itself in the appropriate God-pleasing action."

With bated breath I waited to learn some secret sin my perfect sister had committed! It seems that after college, she and a friend found themselves the only "non-senior citizens" on a trip to the Holy Land. One of their "mutual amusements" on the trip was that these two young women would privately imitate the drooling behavior of one of the seniors, who had suffered a stroke. "I am ashamed to say we took turns imitating this very fine gentleman's

37. My sister and I need to have a discussion someday about whether our parents had age eight pegged as the best year for their children's public profession of faith and baptism!

condition. I have tried over the intervening years to never repeat that kind of behavior, which is certainly *not* pleasing to God."

Jana has not fallen from the pantheon of near-perfect-sisters for me by this admission; and I know that this memory caused her great agony to recall after all these years. Thank you, dear sister, for sharing this with me (and with the reading public for as long as this book is in print!)

My wife, Miran, and I begin most days with these words, "This is the day the Lord has made, let us rejoice and be glad in it."[38] Knowing that each new day "is the day the Lord has made" and that I am "to rejoice and be glad in it," refocuses me to try *again* to "desire to please God." Even Merton agreed that *the desire* to please God is never completely fulfilled; he wants us only to pray for the ongoing *hope* that we never do anything apart from that desire, even if that desire is almost impossible for any of us to maintain perfectly.

Turn It, Turn It, Turn It

1. The Philippians passage "For God is working in you, giving you the desire and the power to do what pleases him" contains our marching orders on how a sinful creature could even dream of *never* doing anything that does not please God. Spend some time thinking about how and when you felt God "working

38. Adapting Psalm 118:24, "This is the day the LORD has made. We will rejoice and be glad in it."

in you" so that you acted in a way that you confidently felt "pleased" God. How does that memory make you feel now?

2. How can you alter your daily prayer life to remind yourself to never intentionally stray from your desire to never displease God? Be specific.

3. Dig deeply into how you would feel in your life journey if you tried to incorporate this phrase of The Merton Prayer into your lifestyle. From what might you be liberated? How might the ensuing hope become revolutionary in your life?

4. Does the idea that "we play to an audience of One" resonate with you? Why? Meditate on just how your life would be different if you focused on pleasing God rather than pleasing people?

5. Is it possible that attempting to please God all the time might in fact very much "displease" some people in your life? Or can you call to mind a situation where pleasing God was in direct conflict with pleasing people? Is there anything happening in your career or relationships right now that has caused you to compromise your walk with God? What are you going to do about any of that?

X

"And I Know That If I Do This You Will Lead Me by the Right Road, Though I May Know Nothing About It"

Scriptural Bases

Your own ears will hear him. Right behind you a voice will say, "This is the way you should go," whether to the right or to the left. Isaiah 30:21

The Lord says, "I will guide you along the best pathway for your life. I will advise you and watch over you." Psalm 32:8

Your word is a lamp to guide my feet and a light for my path. Psalm 119:105

Your road led through the sea, your pathway through the mighty waters—a pathway no one knew was there! Psalm 77:19

Show me where to walk, for I give myself to you. Psalm 143:8

God is my strong fortress, and he makes my way perfect. He makes me as surefooted as a deer, enabling me to stand on mountain heights. 2 Samuel 22:33-34

Exegesis

The "I know" of this phrase is very different than the "I hope" of the previous two phrases. Merton's hope around desiring to please God focuses on the *human* efforts involved; now with the "I know" phrase we hear Merton's bedrock certain confidence that focuses on *God's* efforts. "I know" connotes a certainty that the desired result will indeed occur, as opposed to the "hope" of the two previous phrases about making the "desire to please God" come alive in our life.

What an honest contrast: "I hope I can do this," "I hope I can do that," and now we get to "I know" that "*if* I do those things" something very good *will happen*. This phrase is what grammarians call a "first-class conditional sentence." Simply stated, the first "if" part is called the *protasis* and the "then" part is called the *apodosis.* If the protasis is grounded in reality, then there can be no doubt that the outcome of the apodosis will occur.

A simple example of a first-class conditional sentence: "If I shovel the snow off the sidewalk, then the sidewalk will have no snow on it." Second-class and third-class conditional sentences are less and less likely to occur; for example, "if I keep shooting 100 free throws every day, then I will be drafted by the Chicago Bulls." Not going to ever happen, totally out of the sphere of reality. What a contrast to a first-class conditional sentence, which asserts something is absolutely going to happen—no doubts, no worries, no fears. That definite certainty is exactly what Merton gives us in this phrase.

"You will lead me" is an indicative mood future tense verb, which means an action is actually going to happen. This phrase leaves no room for doubt. It summarizes in four simple words God's role in our lives. Not "you *might* lead me" or "I *hope* you will lead me;" the message of power is certain: "You *will* lead me." Notice also that the *scope* of the "leading" by God is not limited in any way. It is open-ended, with limitless application to our everyday lives of going to and fro.

And where are those led who desire to please God in all things? By the "right road, says Merton, (as opposed to the multitude of wrong roads we might choose). We fallible humans may often not even have a clue that a certain road *is* the right road, hence Merton's reminder: "though I may know nothing about it."

Finally, notice the symmetry of the beginning and ending phrases in this passage, both focusing on the word *know.* The first "know" is positive, the presence of understood knowledge, the confidence that if I do this you Lord will do that. The second "know" is negative, the presence of the not-understood, the absence of knowledge, honest ignorance. Of course, that is exactly Merton's point: I can have confidence in God's guidance, even while being ignorant of where the road is, where it is leading, or whether it is a safe road I am walking on. As the old commercial for Alka-Seltzer used to say, "Oh, oh, what a relief that is!"

Personal Stories

Every single time I get to the words "I know" in this prayer, my heart is calmed and I always seem to hit the pause button, even for just a second or two, before going on. Why is that? Because the promise of the Lord's action contained in that two-word phrase lifts me to the heights of joy and peace and inner renewed strength. *Yes, Yes, Yes, Steven. You do indeed have the desire to please God in everything you do. That means you* can know *for certain that God is leading you on the right road...even when you* don't know *anything about it.*

As a senior in high school, I also enrolled at the University of Kentucky (UK), since I only needed a few high school courses to graduate. Being a UK freshman allowed me (along with two dozen other UK students, all older than me) to go on a three-month "mission" to Bogota, Colombia, with the International YMCA and the Peace Corps.

One permanent memory from that summer was a visit to a church deep inside a mountain, accessed only by a very long walk through a very dark unlit tunnel. The guide hooked us up to one another and to her, by a rope around our waists, and we ventured in a long line into the pitch darkness, moving one step at a time with each gentle tug of the rope. My eighteen-year-old heart was both excited and terrified as this excursion twisted and turned, upwards and downwards, deeper and deeper into the mountain.

Finally, after what seemed to me two miles (more likely it was 1,000 feet), the guide told us all to stop walking. We stood still in silence for a moment. Then the lights suddenly came on and I gasped with awe at the most gorgeous holy cathedral I had ever seen. I had trusted the guide, the rope had not failed, and the reward of my walking a path that I could not see had paid off greatly. I knew that my guide was "leading me by the right road" then, just as I know now that my Lord leads me by the right road—even and especially when I cannot see every twist and turn of the road upon which I am walking.

In the Appendices to this book, I recall some disappointments I have encountered in my life, including the failure to find a job teaching Biblical languages, a severe career-path change, the abrupt unwanted ending of a job with a law firm, starting my own law firm instead of seeking the security of working for others, and of course the news of my aggressive life-threatening cancer. Each one of those roads were not paths I wanted, would have chosen, or enjoyed traveling down at the onset of each particular journey. However, my faith that God's hand was on my shoulder for each step of my life led me to a place of calm acceptance and strong resolve to move quickly into each new "road." I thank Merton's prayer for giving me that insight.

I was "into" The Merton Prayer long before I even knew of it, much less really *knew* it. My sister Jana shared this quote with me from an unknown author, "God is not only the God of our destination but also the God of our detours." Some of our craziest, disappointing, and even fatal detours in life are actually getting us on the exact path God wants us to be on. Desiring to please God, according to Merton, can lead us to welcoming the "right road," where God accompanies us every step of the way.

Turn It, Turn It, Turn It

1. Have you ever felt God whispering in your ear as the prophet so vividly described in Isaiah: "Your own ears will hear him. Right behind you a voice will say, 'This is the way you should go,' whether to the right or to the left." Think about a time when you truly sensed God helping you (or someone you love) take the right fork in the road.

2. Reflect on one or two "right roads" God has led you down without you knowing they were the right roads for you until much later. How might you find encouragement in this about future roads you must take? What changes might you make as a consequence of this encouragement?

3. Were there times when you had a sense that it was God, as the prophet Samuel puts it, who "makes me as surefooted as a deer, enabling me to stand on mountain heights"? If so, how did that *surefootedness* feel, and did it change anything about the results from your "standing on the heights"?

4. With what or whom might you need to engage to make this phrase of The Merton Prayer become real for you? Be specific.

5. Have you ever felt like God's destination for you involved significant detours from the path you had chosen and were following? Why? Did you get to the end of one of those detours and become convinced that it was exactly the right roads you were meant to take? Name a person right now whom you will share this experience with, and then do it!

XI

"Therefore, I Will Trust You Always, Though I May Seem to Be Lost and in the Shadow of Death"

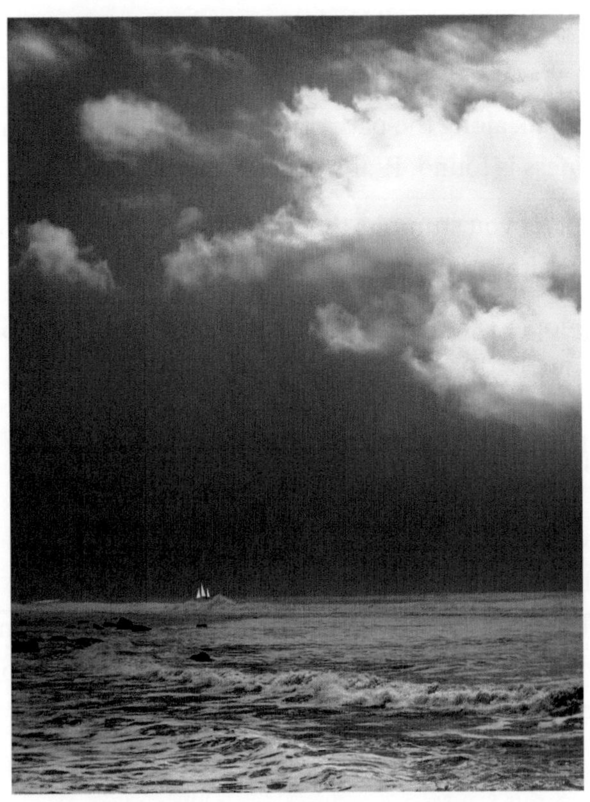

Scriptural Bases

Even though I walk through the valley of the shadow of death, I will not fear. Psalm 23:4

The Sovereign Lord is my strength! He makes me as surefooted as a deer, able to tread upon the heights. Habakkuk 3:19

This I declare about the Lord: He alone is my refuge, my place of safety; he is my God, and I trust him. For he will rescue you from every trap and protect you from deadly disease. He will cover you with his feathers. He will shelter you with his wings. His faithful promises are your armor and protection. Psalm 91:2-4

Make me walk along the path of your commands, for that is where my happiness is found. Psalm 119:35

He will not let you stumble; the one who watches over you will not slumber. Psalm 119:35

Fearing people is a dangerous trap, but trusting the Lord means safety. Proverbs 29:25

Exegesis

The word *therefore* here is a second fulcrum of Merton's prayer in that it takes *everything* that has been prayed up till now and answers the big "so what?" question. In grammatical terms, "therefore" is a resultant conjunction—that is, what went before results in what comes after.

Because of everything we have just prayed, we make the conscious choice to "trust" God. *That* is the answer to the big "so what?" question. *Trust* is an action verb, which involves reliance on faithfulness, with confidence that our reliance is well founded and positive. It is usually, as here, a transitive verb, which means it has a direct object following, and that object receives the action of the verb. The recipient of our trust for Merton is God alone: "I will trust *you*." Merton's crescendo call to action results in trusting God "always," again another all-inclusive word that covers everything, everywhere, always and in all ways.

It has been noted by many that the opposite of trust or faith is not doubt, it is certainty. As Merton says, we "may seem to be lost and in the shadow of death," but it is trust that God ultimately has our back—even though we can't explain it, even to ourselves—that keeps us going.

Personal Stories

"Mr. Denny, I am sorry to report that you have very aggressive prostate cancer." Sitting in that physician's office in December 2016, two weeks after undergoing a biopsy, and hearing those fourteen words, brought me to my first-ever encounter with "the shadow of death." For not a few moments I felt "lost" and the entire Merton Prayer flooded through my brain. As I repeated this prayer to myself while staggering alone out of the hospital, a calm flooded my soul when I got to this "therefore" phrase.

The old adage, "that's where the rubber hits the road," also came flooding into my heart and brain. I had thoughts like these:

- *Steven A. Denny, has your whole life as a Christian been a façade?*
- *You told others that God shows up when we admit we are lost, so do you think God is really going to forget you now?*
- *Surely your trust in God cannot possibly be just for the sunny days of good health.*
- *Yeah, but what if I just have a few weeks to live?*

In those seconds of mind-whirling thoughts about leaving loved-ones, not helping clients across the finish lines with their cases, planning a funeral (my own), and the certain coming pain and surgery, I honestly can testify that The Merton Prayer saved my life. I went home; told my wife, Miran; prayed; cried; and then kept repeating this prayer over and over and over. Calm came with the confidence that God is real, trustworthy, and cares about me, just like Merton's prayer says.

Trust is such a rich word, filled with both happy and painful connotations for we frail human beings. We trust our employees not to steal from us. We trust our government to protect us from enemies. We trust our spouse not to commit adultery. We trust our bank not to steal our money. When our trust is misplaced, the pain is excruciating. In the human arena, is there a human being you feel who is 100% worthy of your trust? That's not an easy question to answer. My knee-jerk reaction is, "Maybe my highest trust in certain humans approaches 100%, but it never reaches it. God alone is worthy of my unwavering and total trust. Merton says that trust can "always" be there—even in "the shadow of death."

A very close friend of mine had a terrible year in 2010. He lost his marriage, his home, his community, and much of his career. His health began to fail him; and he shared with me that he "wept much." This particular phrase of The Merton Prayer resonated in his soul as he encountered the Genesis 12 story of how God called Abram to uproot his family from the comforts of home and go to a new country he didn't even know. The "terrifying" hope of a new life was buoyed by my friend's newfound trust in God, derived from The Merton Prayer, while he "seemed to be lost" on so many fronts.

But even so, trusting God is a whole lot harder when things aren't going all that well. As a pastor, I had many experiences of standing by the hospital bed of beloved parishioners or their loved one, hearing their confident "trust" that simply defies non-Christian logic.

The last words of committed Christians have always stirred my heart and soul. For example, my three siblings and I stood at our father's bedside in 1993, following his heart attack and bypass surgery. We asked Gayle M. Denny if he wanted to endure more surgery and permanent dialysis or if he was ready to be with his Maker/Savior. His response, communicated to us through non-verbal signals, was "Please let me go! I am ready to leave and confident that my Lord will welcome me." That is real "trust" in God, the kind that Merton promises will "always" be there. Thank you, Daddy, for your faithful walk with the Lord, right up to the very end of your earthly life.

Turn It, Turn It, Turn It

1. Trusting God "always" is just about the hardest challenge there is. Can you recall sometimes in your life when you truly felt "lost" or "in the shadow of death?" Did you feel like God was close to you then or far away? Tell the truth. What was the result?

2. What can you do practically to increase your confidence that God is leading you at all times, even the difficult ones. Be specific.

3. What "roads" have you hesitantly started down in the past, only later to become confident that the Lord was leading you by the "right path?" What lessons can you learn from this realization?

4. Take the first passage above from Psalm 23 and personalize it, paraphrasing it so that you articulate the specifics of your current difficult choice of "roads" to travel. Allow the Psalm to speak to you and for you. Voice it as your prayer to God. (For example, "Even though I just lost my job and don't have an idea about what to do next, Lord, I'm not going to let it undermine my confidence or keep me from updating my resume.")

5. Habakkuk refers to "surefooted deer" able to "tread upon the heights." Imagine yourself scaling rough mountains and never losing your footing; how would it feel to have the Creator of those mountains protecting you from all dangers as you climb? (You do, even if you don't yet have complete faith.)

XII

"I Will Not Fear"

Scriptural Bases

Jesus spoke to them at once, "Don't be afraid," he said. "Take courage. I am here." Matthew 14:27

Perfect love expels all fear. If we are afraid, it is for fear of punishment, and this shows that we have not fully experienced his perfect love. I John 4:18

The Lord is my light and my salvation—so why should I be afraid? Psalm 27:1

Yea, though I walk through the valley of the shadow of death, I will fear no evil. Psalm 23:4a (KJV)

"I am leaving you with a gift—peace of mind and heart. And the peace I give is a gift the world cannot give. So don't be troubled or afraid." John 14:27

Do not be afraid, for I have ransomed you. I have called you by name; you are mine. Isaiah 43:1b

Exegesis

"I will not fear" is an all-encompassing, future tense, indicative mood verb, modified with the negative "not." It means that literally there is no place, no time, no circumstance, no remote possibility that "fear" will occur in us. A powerful definitive statement of fact, the phrase "I will not fear" claims victory over fear for the person who is trusting the Lord, even in the midst of life-threatening circumstances. Merton dismisses fear with four words!

Fear is an "unpleasant, often strong, emotion caused by the anticipation or awareness of danger."[39] Simple, direct, with no wiggle room, The Merton Prayer says: "I will not fear." The Greek word for fear in I John 4:18 is *phobos* from which we get our word "phobia." There are indeed fears that psychiatrists and psychologists will label as totally involuntary, but "perfect love (*agape*) casts out fear (*phobos*)," claims St. John. Does this statement apply even to deep-seated psychiatric conditions where medical help is required?

The Matthew 14:27 passage quoted above includes a present tense imperative Greek verb, *me phobeisthe,* which literally means "stop being afraid." Jesus has acknowledged that the disciples were very much "being afraid" seeing him walking toward them on top of the water, and that is why he tells them to "stop it." Even more telling is that when Jesus encounters his disciples after he has risen from the dead he always greets them with "Do not be afraid." I used to think that he meant "Don't be afraid of seeing a ghost," but through The Merton Prayer I have come to understand that he meant "Don't be afraid of anything. I've even conquered death. There's nothing left to fear."

I believe that The Merton Prayer phrase "I will not fear" does apply to both voluntary and involuntary reactions to threatening situations and that this insight can assist doctors in providing medical treatment where needed. But I think the main point is that by his death and resurrection Jesus has shown that there is absolutely nothing left to fear.

39. "Fear." Merriam-Webster.com Dictionary (Merriam-Webster, 2020), https://merriam-webster.com/dictionary/fear.

Personal Stories

Merton's stark phrase "I will not fear" always whips my heart back to the 23rd Psalm, which my mother, who doubled also as my third grade Sunday School teacher, helped me to memorize. I never quite got the concept of a "rod and staff" bringing me "comfort," since my experience of parental discipline involved spankings! But I quickly fastened my young heart on the phrase "I will not fear," since every child knows fear in a multitude of situations.

My forehead still bears the scar of a childhood fall I took into the foundation of a nearby house under construction, only the basement of which had been dug and concrete poured. Peering into the basement while standing on top of the narrow foundation wall, I lost my balance and fell, with a bloody scalp wound the result. I also recall two other things about that day: an older neighborhood "bully" threw dirt clods at me while I lay on the ground, and my brother Gerald came to rescue me out of that basement and took me home to receive first aid care. As a child I simply did not appreciate the danger of standing on such a narrow edge.

"Awareness of danger" was very much on my adult mind years later as I drove my car into the very narrow road leading to the top of Pikes Peak in Colorado, which is over 14,000 feet high. The "awareness" quickly turned to flat-out sheer panic and fear. Once I had entered that road, I could not turn around, nor could I stop and switch drivers; I had to keep driving all the way to the top. To put it mildly, very mildly, I was terrified.

My fear came from the sheer drop-offs at the edge of the road, where there were absolutely no guard-rails. I tried to keep my car as far away from the drop-off edge as possible, but when descending cars approached I thought I was going to have a heart attack, as my right tires were inches from being off the road, leading to falling thousands of feet to the bottom of the mountain... and certain death. After what seemed like hours, when we finally got to the top of Pikes Peak and pulled into a parking area, I just sat there getting my breathing and pulse rate under control. I was absolutely incapable of driving the car back down that same road, and my recollection is that I sat in the back seat and kept my eyes closed while praying all the way down.

I have had a fear of heights, or more accurately a fear of "edges," since I was a child. My parents took us on a vacation, also in Colorado, and as we crossed the narrow bridge over the Royal Gorge Canyon (which is 955 feet above the Arkansas River) my father gripped the steering wheel with ferocity as he sweated bullets, muttering something like, "oh no, oh no." His fear was contagious, and my young heart caught a full dose of it. At the same time, my mother started singing one of her favorite hymns, as this was clearly a worshipful event for her, seeing God's incredible creation. She sang, "This is my Father's world, and to my listening ears, all nature sings, and round me rings the music of the spheres."[40] My mother's pretty voice was drowned out by my father's shouts: "Mary Katherine, be quiet! Can't you see how high up we are?"

---

40. Maltbie D. Babcock, "This is My Father's World" (poem), *Thoughts for Every-Day Living* (Charles Scribner's Sons, New York 1907); set to music by Franklin L. Sheppard, TERRA BEATA (tune), 1915; see https://en.wikipedia.org/wiki/This_Is_My_Father%27s_ World#cite_note-4.

I am sure this childhood event contributed to a panic attack I had in 2008 when I took my youngest daughter and her friend on a spring vacation to Galveston, Texas. After getting our rental car in Houston, we drove east on the interstate and quickly encountered an extremely high bridge. I did not notice how steep the bridge was, nor how short the side guard rails on this bridge were, until after I had left the toll booth at the base of the bridge. Panic set in immediately, just as it had decades earlier at Pikes Peak, since I could not turn around or switch drivers (two 15-year-olds were my only companions this time).

I had to keep going. Up and up and up, at what seemed to me a 45-degree angle, with very tiny guard rails on the right edge. Fortunately, the highway had three east bound lanes, so I quickly navigated to the inner left lane, furthest from the edge! I never got over 15 miles per hour as traffic zoomed by me in the other two lanes. Other east bound drivers gave me the stare of disgust that says, "What the blank's the matter with you buddy?" And/or they flashed the universal finger sign of vile profanity at me and the girls.

My knuckles were white, perspiration popped all over my face, but I just kept going. At one point, when I was heavily hyperventilating, one of the girls tore open a bag that resulted in pretzels flying all over the interior of the car. The girls laughed and sang, and their indifference to my extreme discomfort sent my panic levels higher. A week later, when we drove back to Houston, my daughter Elena said, "Dad, what happened to that crazy high bridge? Grace and I wanted to see you drive over it again?" To which I replied, with a smug smile, "Took a different route this time; sorry to disappoint you!"

Fear is real; there is no doubt that it creeps into our psyches and can lead us into despair. Only through constant closeness with the Lord can my fears ever be calmed. I heard a pastor once say, "worry and worship cannot coexist." I believe that is absolutely true. Merton's grabbing of Psalm 23 here, when combined with the power of the 1 John 4:18 passage noted above, surely confirms that if I am consciously worshipping the Lord I cannot consciously be harboring worry or fears. My mother had it right when she sang to worship the Lord of Creation, and I had it wrong when I only could see how close the dangerous edges were.

For example, my annual income as a sole practitioner trial attorney waxes and wanes, from feast to famine. In one particularly low-income year, I recall sharing with my children that the family's tight budget meant less "discretionary spending" on non-necessary items. I tried to model for my children that my faith sustains me during the times of "famine" when it came to low income. I even adapted a passage from Psalm 50:10 and told them, "Kids, I am not worried about this situation, so don't be afraid, because my father owns the cattle on a thousand hills." My astute, then teenage eldest, Katrina, hesitatingly asked, "Dad, do you mean that Granddaddy Denny owns a farm in Kentucky?" Stifling a smile, I said, "Well, it sort of does mean that, but it's not exactly a farm with real cattle."

Merton pushes "I will not fear" to a place where we confidently state with assurance that fear will not abide and take root in our hearts. When the specter of fear and phobias rise up to smack us, this phrase in its unambiguous clarity and precision can lower the pulse rate and focus us on that "perfect love" of God which is the kind that "casts out fear." How, exactly, can we humans ever live without "fear"? Merton's answer to that question will be found in the concluding two phrases of the prayer: We will not fear because *God is with us constantly* and because *God will never abandon us.*

Turn It, Turn It, Turn It

1. Can you recall times when you or someone you love strongly felt the power of God removing fear from a situation? If so, describe what happened.

2. Meditate on the I John 4:18 passage "perfect love (*agape)* casts out fear (*phobos*)" and think about God's perfect love casting out all fears from your life. How would your life be without phobias?

3. Do you agree with the adage that "worry and worship cannot coexist?" If so, explain what it means in your experience. Be specific.

4. Can you imagine your daily life journey where you claim this phrase "I will not fear," much as Jesus told Satan "Get behind me"? Could this phrase be your "mantra" as fear creeps close?

5. There are deep-rooted psychological phobias, e.g., fear of spiders, fear of heights, fear of edges, etc., which usually keep us from *voluntarily* coming close to things we fear. If you—like me in the driving experiences noted above—find yourself involuntarily afraid because of a phobia, can you see yourself calling on this phrase of The Merton Prayer for solace? Why or why not?

XIII

"For You Are Ever with Me"

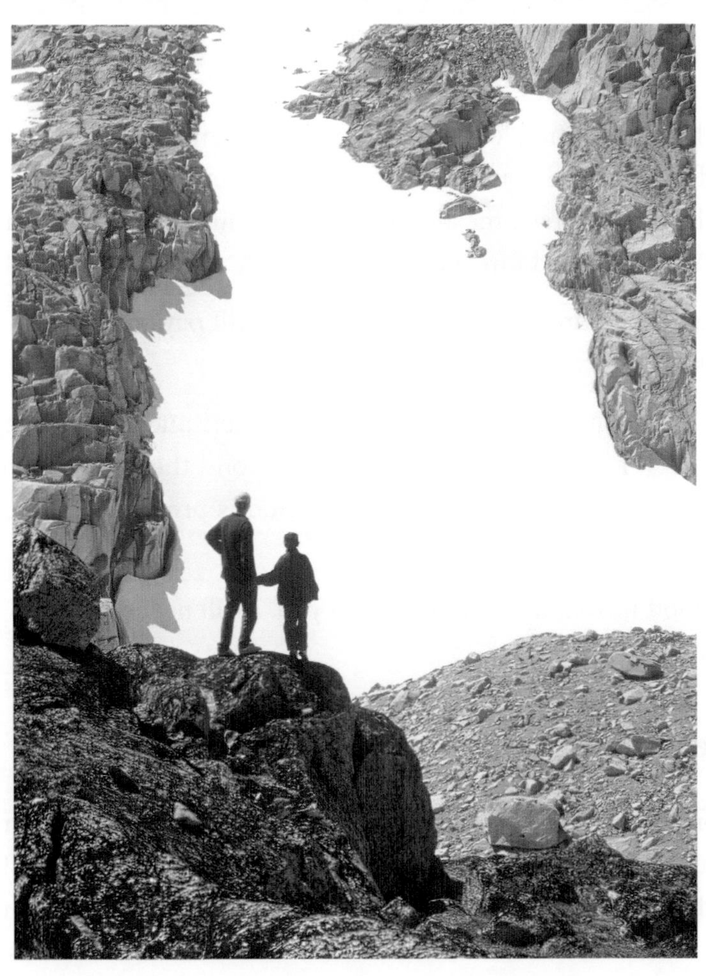

Scriptural Bases

The Lord himself goes before you and will be with you. Deuteronomy 31:8a (NIV)

"This is my command—be strong and courageous! Do not be afraid or discouraged. For the Lord your God is with you wherever you go." Joshua 1:9

I will not be afraid, for you are close beside me. Your rod and your staff protect and comfort me.... Surely your goodness and unfailing love will pursue me all the days of my life, and I will live in the house of the Lord forever. Psalm 23:4b, 6

"See, I [the Lord] care about you, and I will pay attention to you." Ezekiel 36:9

We have a priceless inheritance—an inheritance that is kept in heaven for you, pure and undefiled, beyond the reach of change and decay. And through your faith, God is protecting you by his power. I Peter 1:4-5a

For God has said, "I will never fail you. I will never abandon you." Hebrews 13:5b

Exegesis

Short, but incredibly powerful, this phrase of The Merton Prayer, "You are ever with me," is the definition of the characteristic of God known as "omnipresence." The word *are* here is a linking (or equative) verb, which means that the words in front of this verb are "linked" or "equal" to the words following this verb. "You" is the pronoun for God, *YHWH*, the Lord and Creator of the universe. "Ever with me" is an essential attribute of God, *YHWH*, the Lord and Creator of the universe. Merton is describing who God is: omnipresent. Indeed, we can accurately call God "the ever-with-us-One." Wow!

This grammatical construction means that Merton wants us never to lose sight of the fact that "God" and "ever with me" are inextricably joined—where one is, there the other always is. The word "ever" leaves no room for God *not* to be with us every second of every hour of every day for all eternity (that is, "always"). Wow, redux!

Personal Stories

In Psalm 23:6, noted above, the Hebrew word for "unfailing love" is *ḥesed*. That word so captivated me in seminary that I wrote my master's thesis on it.[41] The usual English translations of *ḥesed* ("mercy" or "steadfast love"), in my opinion, are very weak renderings of this incredibly rich Hebrew word. Indeed, the full meaning of *ḥesed* is incapable of being translated by one English word. *Ḥesed* always involves a *reciprocal relationship* between two or more people, and always includes a *covenant between* the parties. I concluded, and my professors concured, that the translations best capturing *ḥesed* are "covenant love," "unfailing reciprocal love,"

41. Steven A. Denny, "*Ḥesed* in the Old Testament," Lincoln Christian Seminary, Lincoln, IL, 1973.

and "loyal loving-kindness."

So, for me, this phrase of The Merton Prayer always involves the *ḥesed* of my Lord, an immensely powerful covenantal and reciprocal relationship between me and God, whose presence is always available to me, at all times. I felt Merton's phrase, "you are ever with me," profoundly as I prepared for my doctoral qualifying exams at the University of Chicago. I was confident that I would do well enough to pass all of my language tests. The one examination area I was very fearful about was Egyptian history.

The test was administered by a professor who "locked" me in a room for the two to four hours allotted. I sat there staring at the blank pages of the "blue book" that I was to fill with my knowledge of Egyptian history. A sealed envelope had also been given to me which contained my test questions. My hands literally trembled as I opened the envelope. I had gotten to pick the order of my tests, and of course I had chosen Egyptian history to be my last exam.

The history of ancient Egypt for my exam was divided into three main periods: the Old Kingdom (2700-2200 BC), the Middle Kingdom (2050-1800 BC), and the New Kingdom (1550-1100 BC). I had decided to put all my energy of study into the New Kingdom and had not the slightest idea of anything that had happened prior to 1550 BC in Egypt. (Incredibly stupid, right? Life as a full-time student with a weekend ministry two hours down Interstate 65 into Indiana had kept me super busy, and I justified my lack of preparation with a hopeful prayer that the Lord would guide me to study the one area I hoped would be needed to pass the test. Talk about the sin of presumption!)

It was the Friday before Easter (yes "Good" Friday) when I sat down in the room to open my Egyptian history exam envelope and learn my fate. I was on the third floor of the Oriental Institute and the window was open, allowing fresh air to keep me alert. I opened the envelope and two things *simultaneously* occurred: first, my heart leapt with joy as there was only one single question on the entire test and it dealt with the New Kingdom; second, through the open window came bursting the glorious, robust, beautiful, sounds of a men's choir rehearsing at the Chicago Theological Seminary right across the street, singing clearly and beautifully the opening words of "The Hallelujah Chorus" from Handel's *Messiah*. I am not making this up.

Seriously? Are you messing with me, Lord? I thought. I could hardly keep from laughing out loud. Indeed, God is "ever with me" and for that I am ever thankful. I don't even need another story to tell you why these are the most important words in The Merton Prayer to me: "You are ever with me."

Turn It, Turn It, Turn It

1. Feel alone often, rarely, never? Can you call to mind some event when you or someone you know had incredible confidence that God was "ever with you?" Psalm 23 shouts at us "do not be afraid" because "God is close beside you." Let that truth sink in this week in your routines, which will take on new significance because of that realization.

2. Are you currently in a situation in which you need to be enveloped by God's *ḥesed* (that unfailing, steadfast, reciprocal, covenantal love)? How might allowing God to begin or renew such a "reciprocal" relationship be a powerful positive in your current life circumstances? Be specific.

3. The Joshua passage (". . . the Lord your God is with you wherever you go") is an unbelievably rich promise. How might praying these ten simple words daily affect you for the rest of your life?

4. Make "*you, God, are ever with me*" your new "breath-prayer"[42] as you mediate; utter it silently and repeatedly as you go about your daily life.

5. Have you ever grown tired of someone's presence? Do you think that could ever happen to you with God? Why or why not? Meditate on the promise of Deuteronomy: "The Lord himself goes before you and will be with you."

---

42. "Breath prayer" is a form of contemplative prayer linked to the rhythms of breathing. Adele A. Calhoun, "Breath Prayer" in *The Spiritual Disciplines Handbook* (Intervarsity Press, 2015). See also: https://www.christchurch.us/attachments/CCOB_BreathPrayer_4-28B.pdf; https://www.christianitytoday.com/women-leaders/2018/february/take-time-for-breath-prayer.html.

XIV

"And You Will Never Leave Me to Face My Perils Alone"

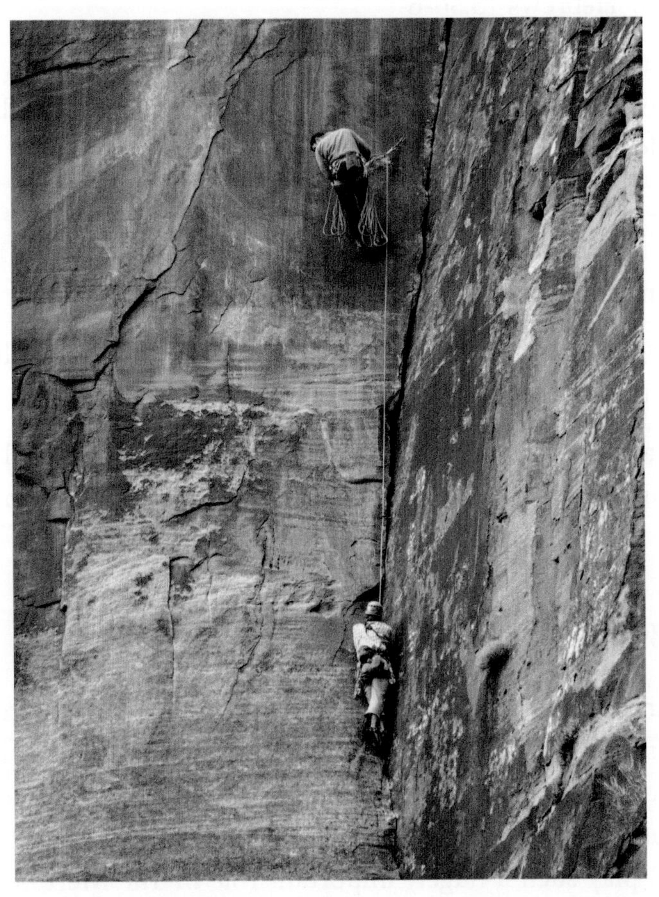

Scriptural Bases

"And I will ask the Father, and he will give you another Advocate, who will never leave you." John 14:16

God has said, "I will never fail you. I will never abandon you." So, we can say with confidence, "The Lord is my helper, so I will have no fear." Hebrews 13:56-6

"No one will be able to stand against you as long as you live. For I will be with you as I was with Moses. I will not fail you or abandon you." Joshua 1:5

For you, Lord, have delivered my soul from death, my eyes from tears, my feet from stumbling, that I may walk before the Lord in the land of the living. Psalm 116:8c-10 (NIV)

Just as the mountains surround and protect Jerusalem, so the Lord surrounds his people, both now and forever. Psalm 125:2

"Can a mother forget her nursing child? Can she feel no love for the child she has borne? But even if that were possible, I would not forget you!" Isaiah 49:15

Exegesis

The antecedent of "you" is, of course, "My Lord God" from the opening of Merton's prayer, thus framing the entire prayer incredibly beautifully. The future tense indicative mood, "will leave me," is qualified by the negative "never." Negative particles (no, not, never) play such a hugely important role in The Merton Prayer.

For emphasis, sometimes in English we place the negative particle immediately after the verb, and I really like doing that here. The question to God is this: Will you ever leave me, God? The answer is so powerful: You will leave me, *never!*

To *face* something means to encounter it directly, without being able to skirt around or avoid it. "Facing our perils" brings us to an archaic English term, but one certainly easily understood by us today (I am writing this at the beginning of the third year of the Covid-19 pandemic). The word "peril" means "exposure to the risk of being injured, destroyed, or lost; danger."[43]

Our "perils" puts us directly before the Lord in concluding this prayer; they include *any and all points* of danger facing us right now. Rather than closing with a prayer for "world peace" (as some Miss America contestants are wont to do), Merton keeps his prayer personal. In fact, look at the entire last part of the prayer and see repeated uses of the first-person pronoun: I, me, my.

"Alone" is the final word of the Merton Prayer and, in my opinion, brings with it the highest level of comfort and real security possible. Look at the concluding three words, "my perils alone," and recall the first three words of the prayer "My Lord God." To me, Merton's sense of poetic symmetry is not to be lost or taken for granted. The man is a genius: Because the Lord God is mine, I will never have to face my perils alone.

---

43. "Peril." Merriam-Webster.com Dictionary (Merriam-Webster, 2020), https://merriam-webster.com/dictionary/peril.

The "crescendo note" of this prayer, as in a lot of great musical pieces, concludes with such a powerful flourish that we are filled with ecstasy and satisfaction. The prayer ends, with no traditional simple "Amen." I believe that Merton purposefully did not end with an "amen" because his prayer really has no ending. It just repeats its power over and over and over. The Merton Prayer stirs both audience and conductor and continues to resonate well after the music has ceased and the crowd has disbursed. At least that is how I feel when I reach the end.

Personal Stories

"Facing perils" in life is part and parcel of the human condition. Some perils we face are minor—hardly qualifying for the use of the word; and some are major—notably injury, death, or loss. Apart from cancer (albeit a big one), I have not faced many truly life-threatening perils. However, one is imprinted in my brain, never to be forgotten.

In law school, my best friend and study partner was Mark Lura, who also had been a seminary classmate and my Greek teaching assistant. We would often zip out after our night-school classes and unwind (both of us had full-time day jobs) by going to see a movie. In fact, Mark and I likely hold the unofficial record for seeing the Bill Murray blockbuster movie *Stripes* more times than anyone else. Mind you, these were pre-Netflix days, and the two of us saw *Stripes* seventeen times, in a theatre, paying full admission price each time. We both came to memorize many lines from the movie and often cracked each other up in class when a professor used a unique word from a funny line of the movie.

One winter night, as we headed out to see the movie again, we were on an interstate near downtown Chicago when Mark's car suddenly spun 90 degrees to the left, then 180 degrees to the right. This flipping back and forth happened several times before Mark got the car under control. I was terrified as the passenger, both hands gripping the dashboard and (according to Mark later) uttering the same word over and over: "Jesus, Jesus, Jesus."[44]

As I type this paragraph, I still shiver with chills down my spine recalling my terror that night. Fortunately for us, no cars hit us and we somehow avoided slamming into any of the close-by concrete barriers. This "peril" was endured successfully, in my opinion, by the fact that I was not alone.

If I had been driving that car, on that night, sliding around on that highway, I would have been far more terrified. I was not alone. The great driving skill of Mark saved both of our lives, and it was nice knowing that I had the job of screaming the Lord Jesus' name crying for help!

---

44. I so identify with the lyrics of the much-later song by Carrie Underwood, "Jesus, Take the Wheel": "Before she knew it she was spinning on a thin black sheet of glass; she saw both their lives flash before her eyes; she didn't even have time to cry; she was so scared; she threw her hands up in the air. Jesus, take the wheel." Brett James, Hillary Lindsay, and Gordie Sampson, writers, "Jesus Take the Wheel" (song), *Some Hearts* (album) (Arista, 2005). See https://www.azlyrics.com/lyrics/carrieunderwood/jesustakethewheel.html.

I get to the end of The Merton Prayer not with an amen, but with the assurance that I, the pray-er, am not alone, never alone. God will *never* abandon you and me to face our perils alone.

Turn It, Turn It, Turn It

1. Are you currently feeling alone or abandoned by God? How so? Are you willing to consider the possibility that your exploration of The Merton Prayer may have actually been an invitation from the Holy Spirit to engage or re-engage with the Lord God (Creator, Redeemer, Reinvigorater, Sustainer) who Was and Is and Is to Come? Why or why not?

2. This last phrase of The Merton Prayer begs this question for your contemplation: When in your life have you strongly felt that you did not face your "perils alone"? Remember or describe it in detail.

3. Read and meditate on St. Paul's statement in Hebrews "God has said, 'I will never fail you. I will never abandon you.'" So, we can say with confidence, "The Lord Is my helper, so I will have no fear."

4. Did you notice how some of your prayers are "generic" rather than specifically "personal"? Take some effort this week to personalize your prayers with the God who will never leave you to face your perils alone.

5. Allow this passage from Deuteronomy, "He will never leave you nor forsake you. Do not be afraid; do not be discouraged," to stop you in your tracks. How can you worry, how can you fear, knowing full well that God not only is ever with you but will never leave you to face your perils alone?

Conclusion

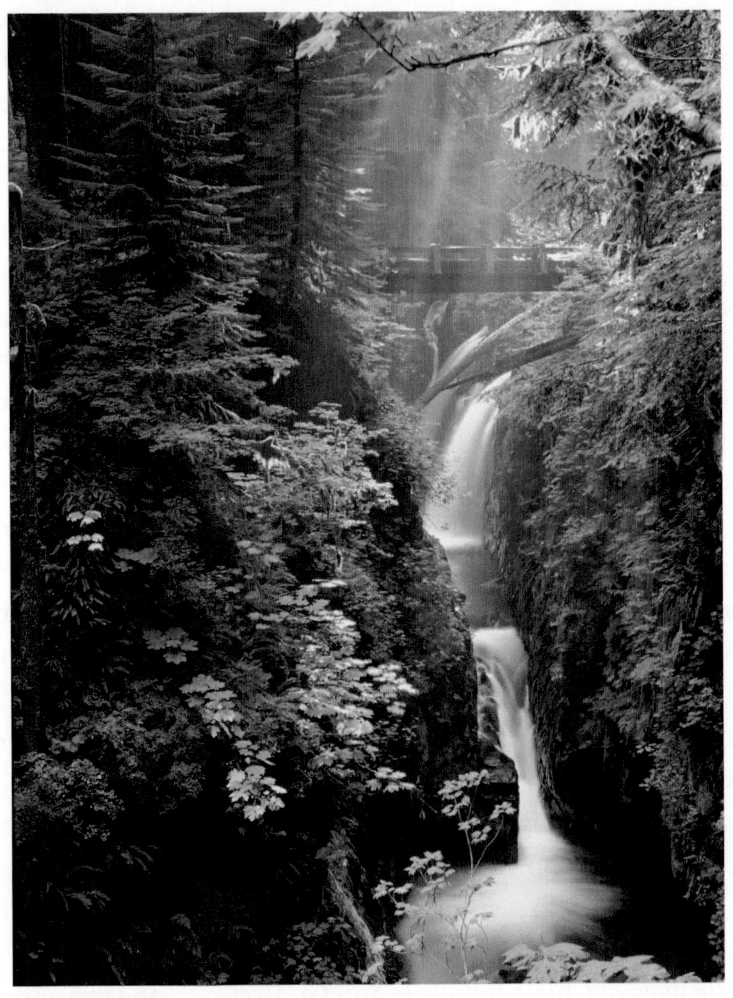

THROUGHOUT THIS VOLUME I have refrained from telling you why each of the Part Two "visual metaphor" photographs by Stephen Hufman were chosen by me, not wanting to interfere with your own entering into the images and grabbing whatever meaning the Lord would bring to your mind. I hope the pictures have been a blessing to you, especially to those of you with well-developed "right brains." I alter my practice only now at the Conclusion to share my thoughts on his photo on the previous page.

Notice how in the incredibly thick forest there is streaming sunlight coming from above. I can imagine that under the dense trees on either side of the raging waterfall there is very little light to see where I am walking. Easily, I can imagine stumbling around in that forest "having no idea where I am going." One small misstep in the forest could lead to tumbling all the way down to the bottom.

Notice how there are no discernible "roads" seen anywhere in this forest, save one: a small bridge crossing a chasm. This "right road" is bathed in the brilliant sunlight. If I could find my way to that little bridge, I would be able to safely avoid the "perils" lurking far below. The "right road" on the bridge is absolutely clear and easy to follow, because of the light shed on it from above; and from whom or where comes the light allowing me to see this "right road"? The light comes from "My Lord God," the Creator of the blazing sun showing me the way to safety.

The Merton Prayer, to me, is a prayer for the ages, not limited to time or place. Once the words of this prayer become real in the lives of Christ-followers and God-seekers, the trajectory of our journey must always be marked by authenticity. I believe we simply *cannot* bring Merton's prayer into our life regularly and remain *superficial* in relating to God or to one another. Superficiality bequeaths superficiality, whereas "depth cries out to depth."[45]

No matter when "now" is, The Merton Prayer is apt and powerful. Humanity has searched for the right road in facing the evils of racial and economic injustice; persistent world-wide misogyny, war, and genocide; and health calamities such as the 1918 Spanish Influenza and Covid-19 pandemics.

Would Merton alter a single word of his prayer for our world and beyond today? I think not. Desiring to please God, honestly confessing our ignorance and weakness, seeking God's leading, and acknowledging God's omnipresence—these are the very things that will allow individuals, families, nations, and humanity itself to choose the "right road."

The Merton Prayer is not a magical incantation. It is a heartfelt, gut-wrenchingly honest reaching out to God and looking inward to view our true and false selves. Every time I pray this prayer, I feel the Lord's hand upon my shoulder, with words like, *Steven, I am so glad to hear from you again, and you know I am always here for you, so don't be a stranger!*

Every phrase of this prayer has Thomas Merton's soul jumping into my soul, connecting me with a monk and prolific writer who was at once a saint and sinner. Given that the original word in Greek for "saint" (*hagios*) actually means "set apart one," you and

---

45. Deep calleth unto deep. (KJV) Psalm 42:7

I may lay claim also to being both "saint and sinner." We are "all sinners,"[46] but as Christ-follower, we are also "set apart" from the world, being "in it" but not "of it."[47]

Every phrase of his prayer has Biblical bases that tie Merton's every word to God's words. That means to me that The Merton Prayer is biblically sound and worthy of great respect, evaluation, and integration into our deepest prayer journeys. Every phrase of this prayer has intertwined with the "warp and woof"[48] of my life in very practical and demonstrable ways. I suspect that each reader of this book could compound the "Personal Stories" section with many personal testimonies of God-led experiences.

As you continue to "Turn It, Turn It, Turn It," The Merton Prayer could soothe your soul and grab your heart in ways you never knew possible; or it might "disturb" your soul and pummel you into more intense encounters with God. The motto "Past is

---

46. For everyone has sinned; we all fall short of God's glorious standard. Romans 3:23

47. Don't copy the behavior and customs of this world, but let God transform you into a new person by changing the way you think. Then you will learn to know God's will for you, which is good and pleasing and perfect. Romans 12:2

48. A somewhat archaic phrase, which I love, meaning "bedrock, cornerstone, basis, foundation, underpinning." Originally these two words referred to two strands of fabric (warp and werf) used by weavers in making strong thread; hence, they came to refer to the "fabric" of our life. Merriam-Webster.com Dictionary (Merriam-Webster, 2020), https://www. merriam-webster.com/dictionary/warp_and_woof.

Prologue" is well known.[49] Civilizations, nations, families, and individuals can and have learned from their pasts so that their futures might not see the same mistakes. Likewise, positive "God-sightings" that are reported and shared with others have a chance to be repeated.

What gets celebrated gets replicated. Your personal testimony of how The Merton Prayer has impacted you can help others draw closer to God through this prayer as well. Share that testimony, don't keep it hidden; the Kingdom of God needs all the words of encouragement we can muster.I encourage you to let The Merton Prayer guide you into sharing how God has led you.

In my volunteer ministry at Chicago's Cook County Jail, I often hear this joyful and loud chanting from the inmates who have gathered to worship God:

- "God is good," followed by
- "All the time," followed by
- "All the time," concluded with
- "God is good."

Can I get a witness?

49. Originally from William Shakespeare's play *The Tempest,* the phrase has come to stand for the theorem that history repeats itself. I first saw these words engraved on the National Archives Building in Washington, D.C. For a history of this phrase, see https://en.m.wikipedia.org/wiki/What%27s_past_is_prologue.

APPENDIX I

Merton and Me

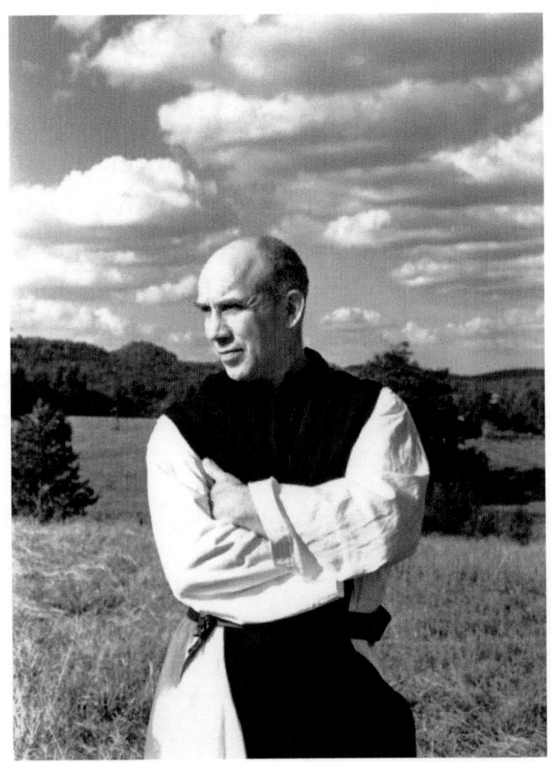

Merton outside the Abbey of Gethsemani

My Very Unusual Early Awareness of the Abbey of Gethsemani

As a native Kentuckian, I had a very strange early awareness of the Abbey of Gethsemani, Merton's home for twenty-seven years as a Trappist monk. Gethsemani is about seventy-five miles west from my childhood home in Lexington. My father, Gayle Denny, was president of Transylvania Printing Company, an office-supply company located in downtown Lexington. The company's accountant was an Irish Catholic who had a serious drinking problem.

My father would regularly send his accountant to the Abbey of Gethsemani for a "retreat," which really meant a time for him to sober up and get back on the wagon. After a few days at the Abbey guesthouse, the accountant would return to work in good shape and thank my father profusely for his generous gift of time at the Abbey. He would bring my father gifts from the monks—some cheese, which I loved, and (ironic gift from an alcoholic) the monks' famous *bourbon-laced fruit cake*, which I hated.

Silent Retreats at Gethsemani

Abbey of Gethsemani, Bardstown, Kentucky

The "drunk accountant" story was on my mind the first time I stepped foot onto the Abbey grounds in 2004. I guess I expected to see a bunch of alcoholic accountants wandering around, but instead I saw monks and serious-minded fellow Christians seeking respite and transformation.

I had signed up for a week-long silent retreat at Gethsemani and was very excited to enter the chapel for the first time. When I sat down alone in the balcony, the sunlight streaming through the beautiful stained-glass windows, I felt the tug of the Holy Spirit saying "Steven, you are in a really, really, really good place—breathe it in and come close to me." Years later, when I read Judith Valente's wonderful book *Atchison Blue*,[50] wherein she describes the unique blue color of a monastery's windows in Kansas, I was jolted back to my first time in the Abbey balcony's stained-glass-colored sunlight. I also remembered how I had walked the grounds of the monastery, crossed the highway, and gone deep into the woods.

During my weeklong retreat, I saw the little wooden shed that Merton described in one of his journals. He prayed in that little shed, found contemplative silence and power there, and dubbed it "St. Anne's Chapel."[51]

---

50. Judith Valente, *Atchison Blue* (Sorin Books, 2013).

51. In an entry dated February 9, 1953, from Thomas Merton, *The Search for Solitude: Pursuing the True Monk's Life,* The Journals of Thomas Merton, Volume III: 1952-1960, Lawrence S. Cunningham, editor (Harper San Francisco, 1996).

"St. Anne's Chapel"

On a subsequent retreat, I was allowed to visit the actual hermitage building where Merton lived the last years of his life. It was a simple, cinderblock structure with only a couple of rooms and a porch, set deep in the grounds about a half-mile walk from the Abbey.

Merton's Hermitage

Nelson County, Kentucky, where the Abbey is located, is far removed from downtown Chicago, where I spend my days in and out of courtrooms. The topography of that rural country (hills, trees, streams, flora, and fauna) is—in my admittedly biased opinion—like so much of my beloved home state, downright gorgeous and a little taste of Heaven on Earth. But more importantly, those Abbey grounds brought to me the birth of a vibrant awareness that God is real in my life. I stood by the grave of Thomas Merton (known to the Abbey monks as Father Louis) and picked up two tiny pebbles nearby.

Gravesite of Thomas Merton (1915-1968)

Those little rocks are on my desk as I wrote the words in this book and, in some mystical way, they connect me to one of the greatest spiritual writers who ever lived. I have since returned for other silent retreats at Gethsemani and hope to spend many more weeks there before I join Thomas Merton, wherever he is hanging out these days.

APPENDIX II

Just Me

Who Am I and How Did I Get Here?

I will now share some background data about me, which might elucidate for you my route to, and my involvement with, The Merton Prayer. I was born in the "Heart of the Bluegrass," Lexington, Kentucky, and I am a "Kentucky Colonel;" no, really, I am! Somehow my father obtained this coveted "honor" for each of his four children, and my certificate is somewhere in my storage files.

Like many Protestant Kentuckians, my family of origin was in church every time the doors were opened—worship twice on Sunday, many Wednesday nights, and youth group activities on the weekends. As a teenager, I walked forward in a church camp to "dedicate my life to Christ" with the intention, not fully understood but full of devotion, of doing some kind of "full-time Christian Service."

High school saw me super active in leadership roles (Key Club, Beta Club, Honor Society) and athletics (basketball and tennis), while also very involved in my church's youth group programs. Not a good enough athlete to obtain a Division-I college scholarship, I followed in my two older siblings' footsteps and matriculated at a Bible College in central Illinois, now known as Lincoln Christian University (LCU).

Bible College and Rev. Steven A. Denny (Weekends Only)

Admittedly, playing Division-III basketball (which I did, for the Lincoln Christian College "Preachers," wearing incredibly short basketball shorts as documented in old photos you will never see), may have been my prime motivation for attending LCU; but once there, I totally fell in love with Biblical language study, both Greek and Hebrew. I did so well in my first-year Greek class that my professor, Dr. Rondal Smith, asked me to become one of his teaching assistants. For the next four years at LCU (while finishing both my bachelor's and my master's degrees), I taught Elementary Greek classes and assisted Dr. Smith in preparing a workbook for first-year Greek students called *Logoi ek tou Logou* ("Words from The Word").

Every weekend, beginning as a sophomore, I drove to southern Illinois and preached for a wonderful small congregation of believers at the Xenia Christian Church. My first sermon lasted twenty-five minutes when I practiced it in the dorm on Friday night, but when I preached it on Sunday morning the sermon was over in eight minutes flat. A saintly elder then spoke for twenty minutes in his communion meditation, beginning with these words: "What I think Pastor Steven was wanting us to think about this morning was...." I hugged the man after the service and promised that my next sermon would at least last a bit longer!

I had been preaching at the Xenia Christian Church for almost two years when the first military lottery draft for the Vietnam War took place on national television. On Monday night, December 1, 1969, many of my friends were gathered around the television in the dormitory lounge watching. Little blue capsules, which seemed like ping-pong balls to me, popped up with birthdates written inside. The birthdate was then placed onto the big board of 366 numbers, starting with #1 and ending with #366 (one slot for each day of the year and a 366th slot for the leap year). My best high-school friend's birthday was the fourth ping-pong ball that popped up. I was horrified for him, since it meant that his lottery number was #4 and he was 100% assured of being drafted.

The conventional wisdom at the time was that any lottery numbers under 200 had a chance of being drafted, while numbers below 100 were certain to be drafted. When the ping-pong ball popped up for my birthday, February 21st, I was totally taken aback. My lottery number was #363. I spoke immediately by phone with my parents and heard my mother's soft cries of relief. I will never forget the ever-present wit of my father: "Well son, that means the Viet Cong will have to invade Frankfort, Kentucky, before you get called up!"[52]

I have spent not an insignificant amount of time reflecting on how my life would have gone if the "road" of the Vietnam War had been one of my journeys. Believe me when I say that "survivor's

---

52. I heard the comedian Robin Williams once say that his father had also stated something similar since Robin's draft lottery number was also very high. As far as I know, my and Mr. Williams' fathers never knew each other, so I maintain that my dad's line is original and came from the pure relief he felt on December 1, 1969. [For mention of Williams' high draft number, see Gene Siskel, "Robin in Control," *Chicago Tribune*, January 10, 1988, https://www.chicagotribune.com/news/ct-xpm-1988-01-10-8803210392-story.html.]

guilt" is real, especially given the fact that many young men from that first lottery draft never made it home alive, and many who made it home were damaged psychologically for their entire lives.

As an ordained clergy in the Church of Christ/Christian Church (non-denominational),[53] I was a pastor for ten years—two at the Xenia Christian Church in Xenia, Illinois, and eight at two Indiana congregations (the Palestine Christian Church in Wolcott and the nearby Reynolds Christian Church in Reynolds). The Indiana churches were about ten miles apart, but they were in two different time zones (that's Indiana for you). The proximity of the two churches allowed me to preach at one and then drive to the other where I delivered the same sermon.

Preaching simultaneously for two churches gave me some interesting experiences. One Sunday, a visiting family appeared in the sanctuary of the Palestine Church, and they sat in the back row. After the service, the father told me they were traveling from Kansas to New York and needed funds for food and gas. I gave them a voucher for $25 worth of gas and food (quite a significant amount in the 1970s, given the low price of gas) and wished them God's blessings.

I then drove the ten miles to the Reynolds church and watched as the same family walked in during the song service and was seated, again, in the back row. At the conclusion of the service, the father again made the same request for gas and food, while

53. Associated with The Restoration Movement, a 19th century American Protestant movement characterized by locally autonomous congregations, which has a goal of "restoring New Testament Christianity."

not seeming to recognize me. As I gave him a second voucher, I could not resist asking him if they had by chance stopped at the Palestine Church earlier, and he emphatically lied "no."

The parishioners standing nearby chuckled as they heard me say, "That's too bad, because I have heard that the Palestine Christian Church pastor is a wonderful guy and I'm sure he would have helped you!" The man took his second voucher, thanked me, and evidently never realized that the same pastor had just given him two vouchers, but I caught a smile on his wife's face as they walked out, so I suspect that she enlightened him later. I often wondered if he did or did not notice that he had heard the exact same sermon twice. I hope at least it was a good one that Sunday.

My life as a young pastor lasted ten years. I enjoyed preaching and teaching God's word, encouraging worshippers, performing weddings, making hospital calls, and actually doing some pastoral care with members of the congregations; but hospital calls revealed a weakness that I was not prepared for as I stood at the nursery window between the new mom and dad, so happy to share with their pastor the excitement of their first-born son. When the nurse carried the child to the window for us to have a closer look, however, the only thing my eyes focused on was the blackened umbilical cord, cauterized by the doctor during delivery. I passed out and fell to the floor while the mom and dad, totally shocked at my reaction, helped revive me. I often wondered if my "pastoral call" had done more harm than good in that instance.

I recall jokingly asking the churches I served, "Please, if any of you must die, could you please die on a weekday so we can schedule your funeral on the weekend when I am already here!"

Amazingly, in ten years of serving three churches every weekend, many funerals did occur, but not a single time did I ever preach at a weekday funeral.

As a young minister in my twenties, it was a natural fit for me to actively work with the churches' youth groups. I also often would get involved with the local high school sports teams and pray with and for the players and coaches before games. I truly loved my ten years as a pastor, and I currently still enjoy preaching with a jail ministry team and occasionally at local churches.

Lincoln Christian Seminary, Illinois State University, and the University of Chicago

My academic preparation to "become a Bible scholar" kept me busy in four different academic settings: a Bible college, a seminary, and two graduate schools. The one "constant" during those years had been my weekend ministry of teaching and preaching in local churches. After completing my bachelor's in Christian Ministry, I earned a master of arts in Old Testament Studies at the Lincoln Christian Seminary, writing my thesis on the amazing Hebrew word *ḥesed,* usually translated "steadfast love."[54]

I took every language class the seminary offered, which ordinarily meant Greek and Hebrew. A classmate and I convinced Professor John Ralls to also offer Aramaic and the cuneiform language Akkadian. We were the only students in those classes, and

---

54. Steven A. Denny, "*Ḥesed* in the Old Testament," Lincoln Christian Seminary, Lincoln, IL, 1973.

we truly loved that special time with such an amazing and brilliant professor.

Simultaneously, I was a teaching assistant at nearby Illinois State University (ISU—Bloomington/Normal, Illinois) in the history department. While there, I earned a second master of arts, this time in Ancient Near Eastern Archeology. My thesis at ISU investigated the archeological excavations at the amazing Old Testament town where Joshua "fit the battle of Jericho" and "the walls came a-tumblin' down."[55]

I was accepted into the doctoral program at the University of Chicago's Department of Near Eastern Languages in 1974, which was housed in the world-class museum known as the Oriental Institute. After four years of intense course work, I successfully passed the qualifying examinations and was admitted to candidacy for the PhD program in Northwest Semitic Philology. I enjoyed courses in numerous esoteric, ancient, Near Eastern languages, which took me far beyond Biblical Greek and Hebrew (*viz.*, Aramaic, Syriac, Ugaritic, Hittite, Assyrian, Akkadian, Babylonian, Sumerian, Phoenician, and Punic).

My major was in the Syriac language, known as Christian Aramaic. I was writing my PhD dissertation under Dr. Arthur Vööbus, a renowned Syriac scholar and Lutheran pastor, whose expertise included actually finding ancient Biblical manuscripts in his regular trips to monasteries in the near east. My dissertation

---

55. Steven A. Denny, "The Alpha and Omega of *Tell-es-Sultan* (Jericho): A Case Study In Ancient Near Eastern Historiography," Illinois State University, Bloomington, IL, 1974.

was to be a critical translation of a never-before-seen 11th-century Syriac commentary on the book of Deuteronomy that Dr. Vööbus had personally discovered. The "road" to complete the PhD took quite an unexpected turn, as will be seen below, and I remain to this day an "ABD" (all but dissertation) student at the University of Chicago.

"Go Get Steve, Maybe He Can Read It!"

I never knew any of my four grandparents, they all died before I was born. My father's roots were in central Kentucky; both of his parents had been raised on farms a half hour north of Lexington. My mother's ancestors, on the other hand, presented quite the intriguing mystery. Her mother, also a Kentucky native, was totally Irish, with long beautiful red hair and the name Rose O'Hare. It's my maternal grandfather's roots that brought the mystery that became an incredible, to me "God-birthed," nexus in my life.

Before I explain the mystery, just think for a moment, how unusual it was for a *goy* (the standard Jewish/Yiddish term for a gentile) from Kentucky to end up immersed in graduate studies in Hebrew and the Old Testament. I was totally "head over heels" in love with Semitic languages, had been since the first class in Hebrew in seminary under Professor Ralls. Sometimes I wonder if my initial fascination with Hebrew may simply have been learning a unique language, which used different characters and read "backwards" from right to left. Awareness that I was reading the original words that Moses and David had spoken and perhaps written themselves grabbed my head and heart as no other academic pursuits ever had done.

I excelled at Hebrew in my seminary course work; I made flash cards and carried them with me everywhere, grabbing every chance to memorize new vocabulary words. When I got to the graduate classes in advanced Hebrew at the Oriental Institute of the University of Chicago, I had some funny encounters with my professors. One would ask me to read the Hebrew text out loud, often adding some reference to my southern accent. One day I asked, "Are you making fun of my accent?" to which he replied, "Mr. Denny, I have never before heard the Masoretic Text read with a southern drawl, and I truly love hearing you read Hebrew."

In December of 1981, my mother's brother, Harry Robinson, died. Uncle Harry was eighteen years older than my mother and had been the United States Postmaster in Signal Mountain, Tennessee. I loved Uncle Harry and have fond memories of his taking my brother and me to Fat Man's Squeeze, where we climbed through rock formations in a state park on Lookout Mountain near Chattanooga. I did not know much about Uncle Harry's life, other than his job at the post office and that he was a veteran who had fought in Cuba during "The War of 1912."[56]

---

56. This little known "war" found American troops fighting in Cuba to assist the government against a revolt by "Afro-Cubans." It has also been called, "The Armed Uprising of the Independents of Color," "The Little Race War," and "The War of 1912" (perhaps a play on the more famous and much larger War of 1812). See https://en.wikipedia.org/wiki/ Negro_Rebellion.

I traveled from Chicago to Tennessee for the funeral, and after the service we all went to Uncle Harry's house on Signal Mountain. The following events are etched into the memory banks of my brain with crystal clarity, never to be forgotten. I am sitting in Uncle Harry's living room along with my mother and her sister Anne, who was seventeen years older than my mother (and only a year younger than her brother Harry).

I heard a voice from another room say, "Go get Steve, maybe he can read it!" I followed the sound of the voice into Uncle Harry's bedroom, where I was shown a shoebox filled with holiday greeting cards. I picked one up and my breath left me: the card was written in Hebrew! It was a *Yom Kippur* card. And there were more, many more, as well as some *Rosh ha-Shanna* cards. All of them had been sent by my grandfather to his son, Harry, who had obviously treasured and saved them.

As I write this now, in the year 2022, a shiver still goes through my body. How do I find the words to describe my emotions? I had a master's degree in Hebrew, had finished four years of doctoral study in advanced Hebrew at a world-class graduate program, had passed my qualifying exams and had just been admitted to PhD candidacy in Semitic Languages. But here I am, standing in my uncle's bedroom on top of a mountain in Tennessee and I had just read a greeting card written in Hebrew from my grandfather to my Uncle Harry!

I walked back into the living room, looked my dear mother straight in the eyes, and said, "Mother, was Grandfather Robinson Jewish?" My mother was speechless; she stared at me with a combination of astonishment, disbelief, and perhaps concern that her son, who was well known to have a goofy side, was just being silly. There were no "goofy" retorts from me, and she saw my profoundly serious eyes searching for my mother to please answer—and to please hurry up with the answer. She then turned, looked sternly at my Aunt Anne, and asked her sister, "Anne, what is Steve talking about?"

My 84-year-old Aunt Anne then told my 67-year-old mother the family secret, which she and Uncle Harry had hidden from her for all of my mother's life. "Mary K, you were so much younger than Harry and me, and people in Kentucky were very prejudiced toward Jews. So, your brother and I decided it best never to let you know that our father was Jewish."

For me, the mystery had been solved as to why Steven A. Denny had fallen in love with the Hebrew language. It's in my DNA. As radio commentator Paul Harvey's famous tagline put it, "And now you know the rest of the story." I insisted that Aunt Anne tell me everything she could think of about my Jewish grandfather. I learned that Grandfather Robinson had left his home in Russia, as a teenager, alone. Perhaps he had fled his homeland to avoid landing in the pogroms of severe anti-Semitic barbarism well known in Russia at the end of the nineteenth century.

Aunt Anne told me that her father had landed at Ellis Island in New York with only a few dollars in his pocket and had gone through the official immigration process. The 1920 United States Census[57] data shows that my grandfather did indeed immigrate to

57. U.S. Census Bureau. "14th Census of the United States: 1920 Population."

the United States when he was only seventeen years old and, drum roll please, his "native language" was listed as *Hebrew*. Grandfather's birth name is lost to us, but his new American name was Robert Robinson.

Somehow, with details not known now, Robert Robinson made his way to south-central Kentucky, where he put down roots in a town called Burnside, near Somerset. Aunt Anne did recall that her father had told her that before he could get out of New York City he had been mugged and robbed of his last few dollars. In Kentucky, however, he eventually met and married the beautiful Irish young lady named Rose O'Hare, and they owned a local dry goods store (confirmed by the census report noted above), which evidently was successful enough to provide for their growing family of five children.

Robert Robinson kept his Jewish heritage secret; apparently it was known only to his wife and two oldest children. Now comes the real kicker in this mystery for me: Aunt Anne related how every Saturday my grandfather told people he was going to Cincinnati to restock his dry goods store in Burnside. Why Cincinnati and not Lexington, which was significantly closer? Aunt Anne, softly and seemingly embarrassed by the words which were to come out of her mouth, recounted, "He went to Cincinnati because it had a Jewish temple for him to go for Sabbath worship."

My grandfather had kept Sabbath worship at the closest Jewish temple, many miles away. I knew that Cincinnati had always had a large Jewish population. Many German Jewish immigrants settled in this Ohio town across the river from Kentucky. Cincinnati also has Hebrew Union University, the graduate program in Semitics where my seminary professor John Ralls had done his doctoral work. I had applied to and been accepted by Hebrew Union's PhD program but had chosen instead to go to Chicago.

Can you imagine how my head and heart were swirling with thoughts and emotions as I digested this story, while reading card after card, all written in the Hebrew language and sent by my maternal grandfather, Robert Robinson, to his son, my Uncle Harry?

Even in this "pre-Merton" stage of my life, I became absolutely convinced that Yahweh had led my grandfather to Kentucky, had led him to marry my Irish grandmother, had led him to practice his Jewish faith in Cincinnati, had led me to fall in love with the Hebrew language, had led me to apply to a school in the town where my grandfather had worshipped, and had led me on a pathway I could never have envisioned—all while I thought I only wanted to play college basketball in a Division-III program!

My drive back to Chicago the next day was mostly silent as I tried to digest this amazing treasure trove of family data. My first day back in Chicago, I told my Hebrew professor this story of having just learned that my grandfather was Jewish. His response was, "Your Jewish heritage, Mr. Denny, will stand you well in your teaching career; and now I know how it is that a southerner is able to speak the language so well." I confess that his comment brought comforting warmth through my entire body.

I Want to Be a Bible Scholar

I was on my way to becoming a Biblical scholar and dreamed of teaching in a seminary or university. In 1979, I had presented a scholarly paper titled "Propagandist *Par Excellance*: *Disputationstil* in Deutero-Isaiah" at the Society of Biblical Literature's annual scholarly meeting in New York City. Possessing what I thought was a strong resume after successfully completing the rigorous PhD qualifying examinations, I applied to a dozen academic programs where Biblical languages were taught.

The only job offers I received were from two universities to which I had not even applied. (I learned later that the places where I *had* applied "shared application info" with *other* schools.) The University of Alaska at Sitka and the University of Wisconsin at Baraboo both offered me a teaching position in their undergrad political science departments. I recall being both shocked and dismayed at this outcome to my dream of becoming a Biblical scholar. The "road" I had mapped out for myself had closed.

I still had confidence that the Lord was leading me on a very different path, but it would have been much easier to travel if I had known The Merton Prayer back then. One of my professors who had written a glowing recommendation letter, upon learning of my total failure to obtain a position teaching Biblical languages, commiserated with my plight by saying, "Steven, I am so sorry, but you picked a bad two decades to try to break into this field." Without saying as much, the thought crossed my mind, *Wait, you guys all knew this when I started here four years ago!* Only my confidence that God had a hand on my shoulder kept my bitterness at bay.

"We Will Pay Your Law School Tuition"

With a Biblical language teaching career not happening and having already resigned from my weekend ministry to focus on an academic career, I took a job in the Risk Management Department of a large Chicago hospital where I was an "Ombudsman" or "Patient Representative." I regularly interacted with disgruntled patients who had complaints about the treatment they had received, which meant that I often found myself "mediating" between the medical/nursing staff and the patients and their families.

My role at the hospital brought me regularly into high conflict situations where my pastoral background allowed me to throw calming oil on the troubled waters of angry patients or angry doctors and nurses. The following incidents are true and involved me as the "on call" Administration representative on weekends:

- This, standing outside a patient's room. "So sorry that we gave your father 100 mg of Lidocaine instead of 10 mg; a purely accidental pharmaceutical inscription error; please forgive us, and please know that our whole team is doing their best to resuscitate your dad right now!" (The patient *was* fine, and the family did indeed "forgive" our error; sincere apologies for human mistakes are so helpful.)

- And this, on a lazy Saturday morning, when called by a frantic nurse. "Mr. Denny, you have to get to the nursery fast, since this resident doctor is about to botch his fifth straight circumcision and I am telling him to get away from this baby!" (The resident was 6'5", the nurse was 5'2", and at 6'2" I stood between them to talk. The resident agreed to let a more experienced doctor perform the circumcision; and it turned out later that none of his other surgeries had actually been negligently done.)

- Or this, when I took the call from a funeral home director, furious with our hospital. "Mr. Denny, your people removed Joan's eyeballs and her husband wants them back!" (I explained to the grieving husband that his wife had legally donated her eyes to science, a fact he was not aware of. All was well and Joan's eyeballs were returned and placed in her coffin for burial, in a jar rather than her eye sockets due to having swollen from the preservatives.)

Getting the patients and their families to accept an apology when it was offered and getting the staff to treat the patients with dignity at all times often presented challenging propositions. Many times, I noticed that my experiences as a pastor came in very handy in high conflict situations. If the hospital apologized for incidents quickly and sincerely, many malpractice lawsuits were avoided. One day, in the weekly meeting with the hospital attorneys and the Vice President of Risk Management, somebody said to me, "Hey, Denny, you're really good at this. Why don't you go to law school?"

At that point in my life, I had two master's degrees, had taught New Testament Greek for four years, had preached in local congregations for ten years, and had just finished four years of the rigorous PhD program at the University of Chicago. The *last* thing in my life I wanted was more education! (A running joke in my family back then was my father's quirky-sense-of-humor-response when someone asked, "What is your son Steven going to be when he finishes with his schooling?" Without batting an eye, my father would smile and say, "Well, as near as his mother and I can figure, he'll be—wait for it—...about 45.")

"The hospital will pay 100% of your law school tuition" was the next sentence I heard, however. "OK," said I, which began my journey to and through law school; and what a journey that was, truly an exercise in "fleecing the Lord" like none other I have ever experienced.

My Multiple Fleeces to God

In retrospect, I see The Merton Prayer all over my life in those years, even though I had not encountered it yet. The "not-knowing-where-I-was-going" is exactly how I fleeced the Lord by not taking practice exams for the Law School Admissions Test (LSAT); not even signing up for the LSAT; being an unregistered "walk-in" where there was only one seat left for walk-ins; not panicking during the LSAT exam when I realized that it took me 20 minutes to read the directions while students on either side of me were already ten pages into the exam; and then—miracle of fleecing miracles—doing well enough on the LSAT to be accepted by all four Chicago night law schools.

I have to tell you that, compared to the academic rigors I had experienced at the University of Chicago, the law school curriculum was "easy." (I certainly hope none of my law school professors ever read this book!). In 1986, I earned the Juris Doctor degree from the University of Illinois/John Marshall Law School.

As a law student, I was allowed, under Illinois Supreme Court Rule 711, to represent clients while under direct and close supervision of a licensed attorney. I spent my last year of law school, working at two law clinics and from both I received wonderful "hands-on" experience: drafting and arguing motions and actually doing some minor "trials" that I only learned later were merely administrative law hearings.

I represented a party in one such hearing, and the opposing attorney asked to speak with me privately afterwards. He said, "Do you have a job lined up after graduation;" I said, "No;" he said, "Your work in this hearing was excellent;" I said, "Thank you very much;" to which he replied, "Would you like to come work for my small firm representing injured workers?" I replied, "Yes, I think I would;" and thus my first law firm position was all set. Thank you, Joseph Hetherington, my first boss as a lawyer, for your kindness which launched my legal career. (This is *not* the guy who was angry at me when I refused to return to court for a trial the day after my youngest child was born.)

Steven A. Denny, Esq.

The doors that opened for me in the practice of law led me to one place, which I believe was always my true vocation: becoming a trial lawyer for the "little person" who was injured. Over the years I also have represented a few defendants, but my work has primarily focused on helping victims of medical malpractice, legal malpractice, childhood sex abuse, and personal injuries of a wide variety. The joy of helping injured victims receive justice has been for me a "calling," much like the preaching ministry was when I was a pastor. (I often offer to pray with my clients before a deposition or trial, and most of them accept the invitation.)

At the bottom of my law firm's letterhead are these words: "*Striving for Justice in an Imperfect World.*" Standing in front of a judge and jury is not at all unlike standing in a pulpit; my new "congregation" is composed of usually a dozen jurors, and my opening and closing statements are my "sermon," hoping to "convert" the jury to believe my client's allegations and to return a verdict in my client's favor.

As I write this at the beginning of 2022, I am grateful beyond words that the Lord has sustained me through thirty-six years of practice as a lawyer, the last twenty-nine of which have been in my own firm. The Law Office of Steven A. Denny, P.C., has always been a solo practice; although I could not have survived without wonderful paralegals, law clerks, secretaries, receptionists, and, of course, the same incredible bookkeeper, Debbie Faber, for all these years. Someone once asked me, "Hey Denny, why has your firm never hired associate attorneys?" To which I reply, "Are you kidding me? I don't trust lawyers!"[58]

During this time of my legal career, I have regularly served in local churches in a variety of positions: elder, deacon, teacher,

58. Jokingly said, of course. However, I have found that paralegals and law clerks were indispensable to my office case load management.

Eucharistic Minister to Shut-Ins, jail ministry, and legal aid clinic. My most recent ordination was as a deacon in my local church, First Presbyterian Church in River Forest, Illinois, where my good friend Chuck Foster wise-cracked after the ordination, "So, Denny, you've been ordained as a pastor, an elder, and now a deacon. Do you realize that you are working your way down to church janitor next?"

So there, now you know me a little better. But mostly I hope you have enjoyed getting to know The Merton Prayer, which has sustained me through all the above turns and twists on all the roads God has accompanied me along.

Acknowledgments

I could never have completed this manuscript without the unwavering support of my amazing wife, Miran Lee. She has loved and encouraged me even when I was most grumpy (on one occasion having seen several hours of my writing efforts not properly saved to my USB drive, never to be recovered.) Miran read each draft carefully and talked me through my ideas before they hit the written page. She has truly lived out the Christian calling of two people becoming "Freely One in Christ" through Christian marriage. Miran said "yes" to my proposal way before she had any idea what "yes" meant. Her "yes" led her to walk with me through three years of cancer surgery, radiation, and hormone therapy. I honestly do not believe that this manuscript would ever have seen the light of day without God's gift to me of my "beautiful orchid" (which is what the Korean words *Mi-Ran* mean).

I also give thanks for my wonderful stepdaughter, Dr. Julie Lee Cheng, whose nightly prayers with me and her mom always lifted my spirits just when they needed lifting. Julie, thanks so much for your undying encouragement and your prayers that my manuscript would find a publisher.

Greg Pierce, owner of ACTA Publications, is an amazing editor who improved my manuscript in so many ways. He has a deep love for Thomas Merton's works and was surprised, as am I, that nobody had written a "deep dive" into The Merton Prayer. Thank you, Greg, for taking a chance on this first-time author.

So many people have encouraged me during my journey of getting this book into print. My longtime paralegal John Hays is not only a brilliant researcher, but as a former pastor he offered invaluable suggestions which especially improved my "Turn It, Turn It, Turn It" ideas. He journeyed with me through every early draft and improved the format and content regularly. John is a gifted writer himself, and I look forward someday to seeing his life story in print.

I owe great thanks to my family members, friends, and colleagues who read early drafts. Judith Valente is one of my favorite authors, and her suggested improvements were extremely helpful. Her book *Atchison Blue* inspired me so much in my healing retreats, and I heartily recommend her other books as well.[59]

Two of my spiritual directors gave wonderful feedback and encouragement: Fr. Dr. Juan Velez (Opus Dei) and Fr. Dr. Robert Sears, SJ. My siblings Gerald Denny and Jana Denny Dickinson both read early drafts of the manuscript and their input was

---

59. Judith Valente, *How to Be: A Monk and a Journalist Reflect on Living & Dying, Purpose & Prayer, Forgiveness & Friendship* with Paul Quenon, OCSO, Hampton Roads Publishing, 2021; *How to Live, What the Rule of St. Benedict Teaches Us About Happiness, Meaning, and Community*, Hampton Roads Publishing, 2018; *The Art of Pausing: Meditations for the Overworked and Overwhelmed* with Paul Quenon and Michael Bever, St. Mary's Press, 2019; and *Atchison Blue: A Search for Silence, a Spiritual Home, and a Living Faith,* Sorin Books, 2013.

incredibly helpful. I especially thank them for allowing me to call on their life stories in two of my "Personal Stories" sections.

My nephew, Pastor Derek Dickinson, not only read and critiqued the manuscript, he also preached a sermon based upon it to his amazing Journey Christian Church in Fairbanks, Alaska. My current pastor, Dr. Paul Detterman of First Presbyterian Church in River Forest, Illinois, read the manuscript, gave invaluable feedback and encouragement, and told me over lunch, "Steven, write the book! This prayer of Merton needs to be made widely available." My other pastor at first Presbyterian, Dr. Allison Lundeen, herself a devotee of The Merton Prayer, encouraged my work with powerful prayer support, while also giving critical feedback on the manuscript.

Two longtime friends and fellow attorneys, Tim Hufman and Tim Huizenga, both spent countless hours dialoguing with me about form and content of the early drafts. Several of my "Personal Stories" anecdotes came from these two mature Christian men. I thank you Tim and Tim—and I apologize for monopolizing many of our Zoom chats with work on this book. Every Saturday morning during the pandemic of 2020, two other attorney friends, Ed Mason and Kevin Murphy, regularly encouraged me at our Zoom "Cutie Pie Senior Attorney's Club" meeting, and Ed waded through an early draft with valuable edit suggestions. Other Christian attorney friends who read the manuscript at various draft stages and gave me wonderful feedback were Dan O'Connell, John Mauck, and Bryan Reed; thanks to you three "gentlemen and scholars" for your edits and words of encouragement.

Several people who had no idea of their influence in my journey with The Merton Prayer also deserve my thanks: Fr. Matthew Kelty of Gethsemani (deceased); Byron Borger of *Hearts and Minds Book Store;* Michael Brennan of the Chicago Chapter of the International Thomas Merton Society; and the spiritual directors, monks, and sisters, at the Warrenville (Illinois) Cenacle, St. Meinrad's Abbey (Indiana), and New Melleray Abbey (Iowa). Each of them were instrumental in my journey with this prayer.

Thanks to my earthly parents, Gayle and Mary K. Denny, whose nurture and encouragement led me to never doubt my potential. I wish I could have shared with them the import of The Merton Prayer; they would have both loved this prayer. They taught me about Jesus and read the Bible to me from an early age; and their joy of life always was infectious. Thanks also to my maternal grandfather, Robert Robinson, whom I never knew. Your faithfulness in keeping the Sabbath of your Jewish faith undoubtedly found its way into my genes in the form of my love and pursuit of the Hebrew scriptures.

Lastly, of course, I thank the Kentucky Trappist monk Thomas Merton. Your prayer has meant more to me and countless others than you could ever have imagined when you sat alone in a private spot at Gethsemani and wrote these words: "My Lord God, I have no idea where I am going.... For you are ever with me and you will never leave me to face my perils alone." Thank you, Thomas Merton, for writing these words, and thank you, God, for never abandoning me.

ALSO AVAILABLE FROM ACTA PUBLICATIONS

Full Circle: A Quest for Transformation
by Juan-Lorenzo Hinojosa and Raven Hinojosa

Grace Revisited: Memorial Edition
by James Stephen Behrens, OCSO

Leaps of Faith: Playful Poems and Fanciful Photos
by Marva Hoeckelman, OSB

We Knew No Mortality: Memories of Our Spiritual Home
by Robert Eric Shoemaker, with images by Sara Shoemaker

Witnessing Grace: Memoir of a Sometimes Subversive Priest
by Denis O'Pray

Where God Is at Home: Poems of God's Word and World
by Irene Zimmerman, OSF